Mental Toughness

Mental toughness is one of the most common terms used in sport – by athletes, coaches, owners, and spectators, and also by the media – however, it is also one of the least understood terms. This book provides a definitive and readable overview of the area, and presents the cutting-edge research in the field of mental toughness.

The book introduces the historical conceptual arguments behind mental toughness research, and looks at the characteristics and development of mentally tough sport performers. It suggests that mental toughness is a personality style and mindset, presenting a case for its inclusion within the positive psychological paradigm. The book also explores various measures of mental toughness and their psychometric properties, and considers cultural and national perspectives as well as the possibility of mental toughness heredity. Sheard exposes the development and maintenance of mental toughness as a factor for successful sport and life performance, and discusses the possibilities for future research on the subject.

This book is unique in considering the idea of mental toughness as an "achievement mindset" and is an invaluable resource for sport and exercise psychology and science students and lecturers. It also provides an important reference for sport participants, coaches, and enthusiasts.

Michael Sheard is a Senior Lecturer in Sport and Exercise Psychology at York St John University. His educational qualifications include a PhD in sport positive psychology. Sheard has published widely on mental toughness, hardiness, and positive psychology, and presented his work at conferences worldwide. He is a Chartered Sport and Exercise Psychologi   with the British Psychological Society.

Mental Toughness
The mindset behind sporting achievement

Michael Sheard

 Routledge
Taylor & Francis Group

LONDON AND NEW YORK

First published 2010
by Routledge
27 Church Road, Hove, East Sussex BN3 2FA

Simultaneously published in the USA and Canada
by Routledge
270 Madison Avenue, New York, NY 10016

Routledge is an imprint of the Taylor & Francis Group, an Informa business

© 2010 Psychology Press

Typeset in Times by Garfield Morgan, Swansea, West Glamorgan
Printed and bound in Great Britain by TJ International Ltd,
Padstow, Cornwall
Cover design by Design Deluxe

This publication has been produced with paper manufactured to
strict environmental standards and with pulp derived from
sustainable forests.

British Library Cataloguing in Publication Data
A catalogue record for this book is available from the British
Library

Library of Congress Cataloging in Publication Data
Sheard, Michael, 1968–
    Mental toughness : the mindset behind sporting achievement /
Michael Sheard.
        p. cm.
    Includes bibliographical references and index.
    ISBN 978-0-415-49109-9 (hardback) – ISBN 978-0-415-49110-5
(pbk.) 1. Sports—Psychological aspects. 2. Athletes—Psychology.
3. Mental discipline. 4. Achievement motivation. I. Title.
    GV705.4.S45 2009
    796.01—dc22

                                                           2009007745

ISBN 978-0-415-49109-9 (hbk)
ISBN 978-0-415-49110-5 (pbk)

For William M. Sheard
(1936–2006)
My inspiration

Tu ne cede malis, sed contra audentior ito.

Virgil

Our games reveal our characters.

Ovid

And courage never to submit or yield.

Milton

That which we are, we are;
One equal temper of heroic hearts,
Made weak by time and fate,
but strong in will.
To strive, to seek, to find,
and not to yield.

Tennyson

Many strokes overthrow the tallest oaks.

John Lyly

The truest wisdom is a resolute determination.

Napoleon Bonaparte

Resolute determination in the pursuit of worthy objects
being the foundation of all true greatness of character.

Samuel Smiles

A cœur vaillant rien d'impossible.

Jacques Cœur

Den Muthigen gehört die Welt.

German proverb

Contents

List of tables and figures

Tables

Figures

Preface and acknowledgements

Mental toughness is one of the most ubiquitous terms used in sport; used by athletes, coaches, owners, and spectators. The sporting print and broadcast media, in particular, have become increasingly preoccupied with "mental toughness". The term is used frequently in interviews, newspaper reports, and during match commentaries. However, it is also one of the least understood terms. It is the aim of *Mental Toughness: The Mindset Behind Sporting Achievement* to help clarify what this construct is and, as importantly, what it is not.

Personality is a meaningful concept and the measurement of it a useful tool. However, there is a growing tendency to put everything that is desirable in terms of personality attributes under the umbrella term "mental toughness". This is misguided and is also a failure to recognize that there are perfectly adequate existing psychological constructs that represent many attributes. It has also added weight to claims that mental toughness is too broad a construct even to consider defining. This is nonsense. The problem is, as it always has been, that it is a phrase that everyone takes for granted: "Mental toughness . . . you know what I mean . . . you know . . . resilient . . . you know . . . digs deep . . . you know . . ." Well, actually, I don't know – until now.

The book is targeted primarily towards psychology, sport psychology, sport science, and sport studies students. The book has been written in such a way that, if desired, it may be read from cover to cover. However, more likely, is that specific chapters will be dipped into. With this in mind, I have written each chapter so that it may stand alone. It is hoped that, having read the entire book, the reader will have developed an appreciation of mental toughness in sport, and will have been made aware of the important advances in its conceptualization, measurement, development and maintenance, and possible hereditary traits.

I have decided to explore the construct of mental toughness in the following way. The book's introductory chapter looks at the anecdotal evidence that suggests mental toughness is a contributory (some would say even a decisive) factor in successful sport performance. The end of the chapter begins to consider situational evidence of displays of mental toughness and suggests that it is a personality style and mindset. This is rigorously extended in Chapter 2, where a theoretical exposition of the characteristics constitutive of mental toughness is given. This is considered further in Chapter 3, which deals with a number of antecedents in the history of its conceptual clarification that have informed its development. It is also in Chapter 3 that the case for mental toughness to be considered within the positive psychological paradigm is presented.

As valid and reliable instruments are essential to the study of any construct, Chapter 4 explores the validation of various measures of mental toughness. Chapter 5 investigates how mental toughness can be acquired and, crucially, maintained. This chapter also examines the research evidence of cultural and nationality differences in mental toughness in sport performers, and considers mental toughness in that all too common band of sport brothers and sisters: the injured athlete. Finally, Chapter 6 offers a concluding commentary and possible directions for future mental toughness research. This includes giving consideration to the genetic inheritance × environmental mediation interaction debate, presently at the forefront of personality theory. Specifically, it is proffered that perhaps, as well as being learned, an element of mental toughness is innate. Perspectives on explaining the attainment of superior sport performance vary, considering factors such as dedicated practice over many years and hereditary contributors. The premise that genetic determinants are as powerful as experiences and environments in life is not new. However, considering the potential contribution of genetic factors to mental toughness is a novel departure. I must emphasize at this point that the suggestion is not one of a pre-determined inherited mental toughness capacity. That would ignore the effect of environmental influences. Rather, it is advocated that research should be conducted to pursue this potentially fruitful orchard of possibility. It is also stressed that it is not the aim of this book to demonstrate an interaction between genetic and environmental factors. Compelling research evidence exists already to this effect. Rather, Chapter 6 acknowledges the interaction between genetic and environmental factors. Whether this interaction is related to mental toughness, or indeed any other key correlate positive psychological constructs, is yet to be determined. Though preliminary findings are encouraging, more research must be conducted if the null hypothesis is to be rejected.

Suffice to say, most readers will recognize the mental toughness mindset presented in this book in the likes of Lance Armstrong, Michael Atherton, Laurie Daley, John Elway, Roger Federer, Clare Francis, Steffi Graf, Stephen Hendry, Magic Johnson, Martin Johnson, Michael Jordan, Roy Keane, Ellen McCarthy, Joe Montana, Rafael Nadal, Martina Navratilova, Michael Phelps, Sir Steve Redgrave, Pete Sampras, Michael Schumacher, Shane Warne, Steve Waugh, Jonny Wilkinson, Tiger Woods, to name only a few. These performers have each done the best they could with the talent they have, because of mental toughness.

I thank Psychology Press for its interest in my manuscript. At Routledge, I thank Sharla Plant, Tara Stebnicky, and Nicola Ravenscroft. I am also deeply indebted to my diligent copy-editor Laila Grieg-Gran. I owe a special debt of gratitude to Dr Jim Golby at Teesside University, for his kindness, wisdom, and friendship. I consider myself fortunate to have been tutored by, and given the friendship of, a true gentleman and scholar. I am grateful to Professor Anna van Wersch, also at Teesside University, for her friendship and tutelage. For their specific contributions, I also thank Shaun McRae, Malcolm Alker, Robbie Paul, and Bert-Jan Heijmans. I offer my sincere appreciation to Dr John Kremer at Queen's University, Belfast, and Professor Arnold LeUnes at Texas A & M University, for their helpful and constructive suggestions on an earlier draft of the manuscript. Their comments were most encouraging. I thank Dr Jim Loehr for his kind copyright permissions. I gratefully acknowledge the pleasant working environment afforded me by the staff at Stokesley public library while this book was in preparation. I extend my appreciation also to the staff at Middlesbrough Central Reference library who were most accommodating in helping me retrieve archival material. I thank Lee West for his assistance in the reproduction of the book's tables and figures. I also thank Heather and Steve Baynton for making my stay such a pleasant and productive one. I thank York St John University for its generous support of this project. I am also grateful to Brenda, Edith, Margaret, and Samantha for your encouraging me to write this book. You know who you are. But, above all, thank you, in particular, to Kinga, and to my mother, Kathleen, for accepting my single-mindedness to begin and to complete this project and for a myriad other reasons than there would be space to list.

1 Introducing mental toughness

> It is not what we get, but what we become by our endeavours that make them worthwhile.
>
> John Ruskin

Introduction

It has been suggested that: "a sporting contest is defined by the pursuit of a victor. Other benefits of a more altruistic and social nature may accrue from sport, but in essence the challenge is set down: to find a winner" (G. Davies, 2007, p. 19). Indeed, our enduring fascination with sport may very well be attributed to "its sole objective criterion – winning" (Moore, 2009, p. S17). Nowhere is this struggle for supremacy more intense than at the very highest competitive levels, where sport is no longer a pastime, run and organized by amateurs. It has developed into a well-established global industry, operating in an increasingly competitive world (Stead, 2003). Sport is a multi-billion pound business that competes for scarce resources and uses, amongst other things, commercial and professional management techniques (Robinson, 1999, 2003). These developments have moved sport organizations toward a more professional and bureaucratic structure (Byers, 2004; Old, 2004; Slack & Hinnings, 1992). In this push toward efficiency, effectiveness, and value for money, it has become of even greater interest to players, coaches, administrators, spectators, and owners to identify qualities associated with superior sport performance as a first stage in facilitating their development. When it comes down to it, there are two qualities that are necessary for victory in any sport: ability and mental toughness.

I am concerned primarily with the latter, though, naturally, each affects the other. The two enjoy a symbiotic relationship. To place emphasis on the identification of ability and a personality style is to subscribe to the view that "sport is neither a moral nor a philosophical undertaking but an athletic and a psychological one" (Syed, 2007, p. 71). Personality is known as a source of moderator variables, and is more likely to manifest in interaction effects, such as influencing the likelihood of actualizing one's ability into achievement (Aidman & Schofield, 2004). The field of sport psychology, in particular, has striven to understand and predict performance excellence primarily on the basis of personality (Miller & Kerr, 2002). Considerable evidence exists within the extant sport psychology literature that desirable psychological attributes contribute significantly to superior sport performance (e.g., Cohn, 1991; Eklund, 1994, 1996; Gould, Guinan, Greenleaf, Medbery, & Peterson, 1999; Greenleaf, Gould, & Dieffenbach, 2001; Hanton & Jones, 1999; Jackson, 1995; Jackson, Mayocchi, & Dover, 1998; G. Jones, Hanton, & Swain, 1994; A. W. Meyers, Whelan, & Murphy, 1995; M. C. Meyers, Bourgeois, LeUnes, & Murray, 1998; M. C. Meyers, LeUnes, & Bourgeois, 1996; Privette & Bundrick, 1997; Thomas & Over, 1994; Vealey, 1994). Moreover, it has been suggested that as sport performers move up toward elite levels, only those with adaptive personality characteristics advance (Deaner & Silva, 2001). This is exemplified by former tennis player Annabel Croft's admission to lacking the emotional toughness necessary to cope with the defeats she suffered in trying to move upward in her sport (Preston, 2008).

At this level, the differences between competitors in technical, tactical, and physical ability are minimal (Moran, 2004). Improvements in diet, hygiene, and medical science have led to the healthiest, most physically robust sportspeople ever known, with, at the highest competitive level, a generation of near equals "stronger, hardier and more resistant than at any time in history" (Goodbody, 2002, p. 32). Physical and technical abilities are more evenly matched at higher levels, so personality becomes increasingly significant, thus demonstrating that "sport is about the revealing of character and inner spirit as much as it is about technical brilliance" (Cleary, 2005b, p. S6). To this end, athletes' ability to focus attention, to control performance imagery, and a total commitment to the pursuit of excellence have been identified as critical psychological attributes (Orlick & Partington, 1988). Undoubtedly, the advice of one of the most successful Test cricket captains holds true: "If you want to improve at your sport, you have to be dedicated, do little else, train hard" (Lloyd, 2007, p. 90). But, ultimately, those athletes with the appropriate psychological attributes make the transition upward because their personalities facilitate the adjustment. The New Zealand rugby union team, the consistently world-ranked number one All Blacks, has an idiom that sums it up perfectly: "It's all about the top two inches" (Loe, 2007).

It is apparent from findings of the current literature that several specific personality characteristics have been indicated that ameliorate sport performance. After reviewing this research, sport psychologists Jean Williams and Vikki Krane concluded: "Regardless of the source of data or the nature of the sport, a certain psychological profile appears to be linked with successful performance" (J. M. Williams & Krane, 2001, pp. 174–175). This general profile cited self-regulation of arousal, high self-confidence, heightened concentration, coping skills for dealing with distractions and unexpected events, feeling in control, a positive preoccupation with sport, and determination and commitment (the very attributes which we will see later are constitutive of mental toughness) as key psychological characteristics distinguishing successful from less successful athletes.

In two separate studies, Dan Gould and his associates reported that 82 per cent and 73 per cent, respectively, of their sample pools (i.e., sport performers, coaches, parents, siblings, significant others) identified "mental toughness" as a vital characteristic associated with successful performance (Gould, Hodge, Peterson, & Petlichkoff, 1987; Gould, Dieffenbach, & Moffett, 2002). Indeed, in the later study, the largest higher-order theme from their interviews was "mental toughness", comprised of raw data responses such as "mentally tough, perseverance, resilient, and persistent" (p. 186). Thus, this personality style appears to be central to overall performance excellence.

However, mental toughness is probably one of the most used but least understood terms in sport psychology. Stemming in part from Jim Loehr's research, it is widely alluded to by athletes and coaches, as well as in the popular media and in applied sport psychology, as a crucial prerequisite of success in sport (Loehr, 1986). Indeed, researchers have felt the need to relabel sport psychology as "mental toughness" in order to sell it to English soccer academy directors and national coaches (Pain & Harwood, 2004). Why do some athletes and teams perform a little better in pressure situations? What separates those who thrive on elite competition from those who collapse under pressure? Why do athletes and teams succeed in the face of adversity while others fail? Why do some performers bounce back from personal failure whereas others are beleaguered by it? Why have some athletes consistently underachieved? Many suggest that the answer lies in mental toughness. According to Jason Robinson, a Rugby World Cup winner in 2003 and an all-time great in both rugby codes, "mental toughness is as important as physical toughness" (as cited in Lynch, 2008). Indeed, it has been suggested that at the highest competitive levels "the essential extra element is mental toughness" and that "this mental toughness needs training just as much as the ability to hit a ball straight and far" (Faulkner, 2006, p. 27). It would appear that to progress from strong performer to champion, the breakthrough ingredient is mental toughness. It is this attribute that allows sport performers to act in an instinctive and automatic way at the most important moments and turning points of a competition or other high-stakes situations. But what exactly is "mental toughness"?

Popular mental toughness

Across a multitude of sports, athletes often attribute achievement and success to "mental toughness". Upon reaching the considerable milestone of a century of centuries in first-class cricket, and becoming only the 25th player in the history of the game ever to do so, Surrey and England batsman Mark Ramprakash said: "I had so many knocks, so many low scores, so many setbacks, and have shown a lot of mental toughness to keep going – despite the blows" (as cited in Kimmage, 2008, p. 19). Also from cricket, of Alastair Cook's second innings century for England against Sri Lanka in Galle, it was written that: "Amid the disappointments, it was great to see such mental toughness from someone so young, right at the end of the tour" (Hoggard, 2007, p. 62). Interviewed on his recall to the England One-Day International side, wicket-keeper Matt Prior reflected: "When you are left out, people give you stick and say that is the end and he will never be back. To come back and perform for Sussex the way I have I am quite proud of. It shows mental toughness" (as cited in Hoult, 2008, p. S20). And upon acceptance of the captaincy of the Australian Test cricket team, the immensely successful Steve Waugh reflected in his autobiography that: "All that was required was the mental toughness to carry out my plan" (Waugh, 2006, p. 52).

Reflecting upon his Olympic gold medal-winning performance in Beijing, British yachtsman Ben Ainslie spoke reverentially of other high-achieving athletes: "The mental toughness of those guys, especially [Michael] Schumacher, was amazing" (as cited in Snow, 2008, p. 32). From rugby league, ahead of a Super League Grand Final victory, Leeds Rhinos forward Jamie Jones Buchanan attributed his team's resurgence to "mental toughness and work ethic" (as cited in Irvine, 2007, p. 79). In praise of their opponent's challenge after his side's third consecutive Rugby League Challenge Cup triumph, St Helens full-back Paul Wellens said: "They gave us as tough a game as any we've had all season. The heat and intensity really took its toll in the second half. In the end our mental toughness got us through" (as cited in Malin, 2008, p. 14). From rugby union, speaking prior to his side's surprise semi-final victory over hosts France in the 2007 Rugby World Cup, England captain Phil Vickery acknowledged that: "We know it will be tough, but I feel we have the players not just with the skills but with the mental toughness" (as cited in Slot, 2007a, p. 120). Subsequently, team-mate Lawrence Dallaglio wrote of England's win: "In the end, it came down to mental toughness" (2007, p. 427). Of the rejuvenation of his international career under a new head coach, Wales star Gavin Henson said: "it is all about concentration and it has given us a mental toughness" (as cited in Rees, 2008, p. 11).

Retired performers have also written of the positive contribution of mental toughness to sporting achievement. Of 2008 Junior Wimbledon tennis champion Laura Robson, former Great Britain number one Annabel Croft wrote of her "impression that she is very tough, mentally" (as cited in Baker, 2008, p. S5). Writing of the positive impact the new national coach has made on Welsh rugby union fortunes, former Wales and Great Britain international rugby union and league star Jonathan Davies observed: "Most rugby nations nowadays are on a par in terms of fitness and technique, but the major difference Warren Gatland has made is mental toughness. It's all in the head" (J. Davies, 2008, p. 86).

Similarly, coaches have spoken of mental toughness in terms of its contribution to performance and results. Ahead of Amir Khan's Olympic boxing lightweight semi-final in Athens, Great Britain team manager Terry Edwards considered that: "An important factor for the rest of this tournament will be mental toughness. This is something that we have been developing" (as cited in Goodbody, 2004b, p. 50). Seeking to rectify a dip in his team's form, Newcastle Knights (Australian rugby league) coach Brian Smith commented: "We need mental toughness to grind out the win for the whole game" (as cited in McDonald, 2008). Reacting to criticism, former Leicester Tigers (English rugby union) coach Marcelo Loffreda countered: "I have felt high-pressure situations with the national side but that wasn't about professionalism, this is. I'll tackle it with a lot of hard work, commitment and mental toughness" (as cited in Hands, 2008a, p. 68). Also from rugby union, Glasgow coach Sean Lineen spoke of injured Scotland flanker Donnie Macfadyen's efforts during rehabilitation: "I've been very impressed, he has shown a real mental toughness" (as cited in Stuart, 2008, p. 85).

Of the England team's change in fortune during the 2007 Rugby World Cup, former rugby league icon and present Wales rugby union defensive coach Shaun Edwards wrote: "Ashton's men had the character, the mental toughness, to turn things round in France last autumn" (Edwards, 2008, p. 9). On retirement from playing Australian Rules football, Collingwood coach Mick Malthouse reminisced: "When a new season starts you tend to forget the agony that you went through, how hard it becomes to get up and running, the cold, the injuries, the effort and mental toughness" (Malthouse, 2008). And from soccer, Glasgow Rangers coach Ally McCoist stated: "It is about mental toughness, a little bit of luck, a certain attitude as well, and a desire as much as anything" (as cited in Spiers, 2008b, p. 108).

The phrase "mental toughness" appears to be used somewhat liberally in the popular media. For example, an examination of the print media, and its respective websites, yields a plethora of reports where the term has been used to explain preparation, performances, and results in a variety of sports: American football (e.g., Berkow, 2006; Hutton, 2007; Reiss, 2006; Tomase, 2007), badminton (e.g., Emms, 2009), basketball (e.g., Goodwill, 2007), boxing (e.g., McRae, 2008), cricket (e.g., Hopps, 2009; Lyles, 2008), Formula One (e.g., Gorman, 2008a), golf (e.g., Dixon, 2009; Reason, 2009a), horse racing (e.g., McRae, 2009), rowing (e.g., Goodbody, 2004a), rugby league (e.g., Irvine, 2008a, 2009; A. Wilson, 2009b), rugby union (e.g., Cain, 2008; Cleary, 2009a; S. Jones, 2008; Lewsey, 2009; Mairs, 2006; Slot, 2007b; Souster, 2009; Stuart, 2009; Walsh, 2007, 2009; Westerby, 2008), soccer (e.g., P. Gordon, 2009; Hytner, 2008, 2009; Kay, 2008; Murray, 2009; Rowan, 2009; Spiers, 2008a; Walsh, 2008b; Winter, 2006), and tennis (e.g., Bierley, 2009; Cash, 2008; Mulvenney, 2007). The following are examples of the term's appeal in the sporting media: "England's . . . mental toughness took them to a famous victory" (Walsh, 2008a, p. 2); "Wasps, the champions, are the benchmark for any aspiring team, for their mental toughness, and their sheer cussedness" (Cleary, 2008, p. S12); "Wenger praised the grit and determination of his young side, pinpointing their mental toughness" (Dall, 2007); "Gordon Strachan insisted yesterday that Scotland's players possess the mental toughness required to finish their Euro 2008 qualifying job" (P. Gordon, 2007, p. 96); "a common trait in all the champions . . . including Prost, Senna, Michael Schumacher and Mika Hakkinen, has been an immense mental toughness. They all had the willpower to burn . . . the difference between winning and losing" (Garside, 2008, p. 15); and, most recently from rugby league's 2008 Super League Grand Final, "a tactical triumph and a glorious vindication of Leeds' mental toughness to recover from their mauling by Saints in the qualifying semi-final two weeks earlier" (Irvine, 2008b).

However, what constitutes mental toughness as reported in the popular media comes in various guises. Several other terms and phrases are used interchangeably to describe those characteristics that are constitutive of popular mental toughness. The annals of sporting history are chronicled with examples of memorable encounters, where the determinant of success has been attributed anecdotally to performers' "mental strength" (e.g., Atherton, 2003; Barnes, 2003, 2005; Coe, 2004; Conquering Heroes, 2003; Corry, 2007; Coward, 2006; G. Davies, 2007; Hayward, 2003, 2005; Hill, 2008; Nicholas, 2007; Tongue, 2008; Warne, 2008; Winter, 2005), or performance failure blamed on its absence (e.g., Bolton, 2008; S. Hughes, 2008; Randall, 2008; Rich, 2008; Winter, 2007). For example, former Formula One world champion Damon Hill suggested of the 2008 champion, and youngest ever winner of the drivers' championship, Lewis Hamilton: "What Hamilton has proved this year more than anything else is that he has huge mental strength" (Hill, 2008, p. 3). Former England cricket coach Duncan Fletcher wrote of the "mentality", "mindset", and "mentally tough" requisites for a successful tour of India (Fletcher, 2008, p. 9), while Arsenal soccer coach Arsène Wenger sought to explain a surprise reversal in terms of his team's being "not completely there on the mental side" (as cited in Rich, 2008, p. S2). Oftentimes, the media use words such as "grit", "determination", and "belief" to describe behaviours constitutive of mental toughness; for example: "Having been given little or no chance against an apparently peerless St Helens, Leeds achieved back-to-back league champion-ships . . . with a performance in last night's Super League Grand Final that examined their reservoirs of self-belief and gritty determination and found them overflowing" (Patrick, 2008).

Similarly, sporting achievement has been credited with coaches who built up a psychology of winning by concentrating on their team's strengths, while failure is due, in part, to adoption of the mentality of defeat (Anthony, 2007). Thus, when the England national soccer team lost at home in its final qualification match and, as a consequence, failed to reach the 2008 European Cham-pionships, the pens (and laptops) were ready: "The quality Croatia possess in particular abundance is self-belief . . . England players may need to find greater mettle on their travels" (Winter, 2007,

p. S2); while "players' state of mind" (as cited in J. Wilson, 2007, pp. S2–S3) and "some sort of mental block" (as cited in Jenson, 2007, p. 2) were suggested by the highly successful, and new England soccer coach, Fabio Capello.

Each of the aforementioned anecdotal explanations is related by a synonymous theme: "mental toughness" (or lack of), and its assumed constitutive characteristics, was a contributory variable partly responsible for performers' success or loss. Additional examples of phrases used synonymously to infer mental toughness include "mentally strong" (Boycott, 2009; Keohane, 2006), "resilient" (Dickinson, 2009; Hands, 2008b; Kitson, 2008; A. Wilson, 2008, 2009a), "mentally resilient" (Booth, 2008), "resolve" (M. Hughes, 2008); "mental resolve" (Smithies, 2007), "resolutely determined" (Irvine, 2008c), "backbone" (Brown, 2008b), "spine" (Ogden, 2008), "steeliness" (Lewis, 2008), "strength of mind" (Parkinson, 2005), "character" (Atherton, 2009; Cleary, 2009b; Pringle, 2009), "tougher character" (Atherton, 2008), and, in particular, "resilience" (Barnes, 2009; Brown, 2007, 2008a; Chadband, 2009; Firfield, 2009; Hansen, 2008; Inverdale, 2007; Kitson, 2009; Ley, 2007; Roper, 2007; E. Smith, 2009; Syed, 2009a; The England Cricket Team, 2005; J. Wilson, 2009). Seven-times Formula One world champion Michael Schumacher was renowned for his "mind games" and, for many observers and commentators of sport, is the epitome of mental toughness (see Cashmore, 2002; Goodbody, 2002). Yet, occasionally, it was known for the tables to be turned, in particular when he came up against Jacques Villeneuve. Of his battles with the French-Canadian driver, it was noted that: "The disconcerting thing for him [Schumacher] about Villenueve was that he was a tough character, mentally very strong" (J. Allen, 2007, p. 189). To highlight further the observation of terms used synonymously with mental toughness, I draw on the print media's coverage of three recent high-profile sporting events: the 2003 Rugby World Cup, the 2005 Ashes cricket series, and the 2007 Rugby World Cup.

The 2003 Rugby World Cup

Of England's 2003 Rugby World Cup triumph, reflections included: "The task of beating Australia in a World Cup final in

Australia needed a colossal mental shift. The England rugby union side has certainly made one: and it was enough . . . Now they are world champions and that represents a serious shift of attitude" (Barnes, 2003, p. 38); "Observers . . . were forced to admit that their own Wallabies had been beaten in a thrilling contest by a more skilful and resolute side" (R. Williams, 2003, p. 2); "Woodward never talked of England doing their best or of them trying to get to the final. He spoke of winning the damn thing from the start . . . His achievements with England have come about because Woodward understands winning. He has a clear purpose and, perhaps most important of all, vigorous self-belief. His absolute determination that he is on the right path, and doing the right thing, gave him the courage to push for what he believed England needed in order to be the best" (Kervin, 2003, p. 36). Paying tribute to the victors, Australia captain George Gregan said: "They [England] are very professional, do what they have to do to get victories . . . That's why they are world champions . . . They delivered under pressure and delivered when it counted" (as cited in Souster, 2003, p. 35).

The 2005 Ashes cricket series

This memorable sporting encounter provided many observations: "Their [the cricketers'] play is . . . psychologically gruesome in its exposure of character" (Nicholas, 2005, p. VI); "Australian cricketers are like cockroaches. You can damage their legs, cuff them on the head and poison their knees, but you can't crush them. Their spirit is unbreakable" (S. Hughes, 2005a, p. VI); "Character. That's what got England over the line. Muscle, at such tense moments, turns to jelly. Only inner self-belief can hold the body together" (S. Hughes, 2005b, p. VII); "Pietersen, mentally strong enough to absorb the immensity of the occasion without being cowed" (Ellis, 2005, p. V); "He [Pietersen] is a belligerent individual. He is cocky and confident; there is a touch of arrogance about him. All the great players have had self-confidence and self-belief" (Boycott, 2005, p. S6). England cricketer Kevin Pietersen himself stated: "In the over against Brett Lee it was either me or him and I backed myself to succeed" (as cited in Hoult, 2005,

p. S5). While team-mate Marcus Trescothick reflected: "Fighting back from adversity is what we have done so well recently" (as cited in Pringle, 2005, p. II).

The 2007 Rugby World Cup

And, from coverage of the 2007 Rugby World Cup tournament: "On the field they [South Africa] had the backbone to win under pressure. Off it, their shirt buttons were done up, their ties on straight, shoes polished. They looked like a team who were proud of what they had achieved. In short, they looked like world champions" (Greenwood, 2007, p. S14); "They [England] made the quarter-finals . . . sustained by courage, coolness and sheer bloody-mindedness" (Rees, 2007, p. 4); "A triumph against the odds, a stunning turn of events, one that speaks of many things: of inner strength, of fortitude, of togetherness, of bloody-mindedness and of duty" (Cleary, 2007, p. S2); "This team [England] has got where it has through commitment, hard work, courage and a desire to prove people wrong" (Souster, 2007, p. 72); "It's what you do when it matters most . . . You have no duty to entertain, if people cannot find inspiration or compulsion from your courage, fortitude and honesty, it's their problem, not yours" (Moore, 2007, p. S3). What emerges is a constellation of desirable personality attributes, each a reflection of mental toughness. The key characteristics identified from these quotes are summarized in Table 1.1.

Clearly, these encounters provided fertile ground for journalists' and performers' comments. Writing after the Australian cricket team's dramatic second Test victory in December 2006 against England in Adelaide, one newspaper journalist stated: "They turned an apparently lost cause into a triumph" (Roebuck, 2006, p. 57). Of one performer's individual impact on the match, the same correspondent added: "Shane Warne's contribution counts amongst the mightiest of his career. Pounded by the batsmen and berated by the critics after a lacklustre showing in the first innings, he produced a stirring performance . . . But it is not only about skill. Greatness is a state of mind . . . A lesser man might have wilted. Not Warne. Instead, he wanted to make amends and

Table 1.1 Characteristics identified anecdotally from the print media as contributory to sporting achievement

2003 Rugby World Cup	2005 Ashes cricket series	2007 Rugby World Cup
Colossal mental shift	Exposure of character	Backbone to win under pressure
Serious shift of attitude	Unbreakable spirit	Proud
Resolute	Character	Look like World Champions
Understand winning	Inner self-belief	Courage
Clear purpose	Mentally strong	Coolness
Vigorous self-belief	Belligerent	Bloody-mindedness
Absolute determination	Touch of arrogance	Inner strength
Courage	Self-confidence	Fortitude
Professional	Self-belief	Togetherness
Do what you have to	Backing oneself to succeed	Duty
Deliver under pressure	Fighting back from adversity	Commitment
Deliver when it counts		Hard work
		Desire to prove people wrong
		What you do when it matters most
		Honesty

convinced himself it could be done" (Roebuck, p. 57). The manner of Australia's victory was profound. I stayed up through the early hours of the morning at home in England to watch the final day's play. I just had a feeling that the game was not going to end in a draw, as most pundits were predicting. The circumstances on the morning of the fifth day were intriguingly poised: one side was playing for the draw (England); the other (Australia) could win. As it transpired, the latter prevailed. Why? Mindset. On that day, in that particular situation, England did not have it. Australia turned up to the ground with the right mindset. I attributed the manner of the triumph to: "You have a plan, stick to it (self-belief), execute it (determination), and impose your will on the opposition to secure your desired outcome (unyielding attitude). Two words – mental toughness" (Sheard, 2006, p. 18).

Such desirable psychological attributes, or lack of them, have been offered as explicative reasons for high profile sporting triumphs and failures. Interestingly, growing public awareness and acknowledgement of the potential influence of psychological factors on sport performance has prompted sufficiently motivated readers to write to newspapers' editors. Reasons for success include: "a determination to imbue his team-mates to believe in their ability to win" (Barlow, 2006, p. S17). Among those suggested for failure: "They [England] do not have the mental capabilities to win consistently around the world in all conditions . . . get a lesson on mental toughness" (Ryan, 2005, p. S10); and "At the highest level, victory and defeat are often attributed to an athlete's mental toughness . . . Rusedski exploded and Andy Roddick capitalised" (Sheard, 2003, p. 25). Evidently, people are thinking increasingly about sporting success and failure in terms of the possession or absence of mental toughness as a contributory factor.

Winning and losing

So it would appear, anecdotally at this stage, that there exists an awareness of the psychological attributes considered contributory to sporting success. But does such success equate only with winning? Rudyard Kipling may have exhorted individuals to meet with the twin impostors of triumph and disaster just the same. Yet, it is probably unrealistic to expect athletes to deal with winning and losing in an equivalent manner. As mentioned at the beginning of this book's introduction, a sporting event is a struggle for supremacy in which every athlete and coach seeks to emerge victorious. Thus, it would be naïve to assert that winning is not an important part of sport. Indeed, as was put to me recently by a professional rugby league footballer, "why keep a scoreboard if the score does not matter?" (Alker, personal communication, November 28, 2007). In a similar vein, Welsh rugby union great Gerald Davies wrote: "Competition is a selfish taskmaster and winning is the exclusive and unshareable gift" (G. Davies, 2003, p. 36).

However, while it is agreed that winning is an inherent part of competition, and therefore an important aim, it has been argued that it is not the only, or most important, objective (Martens, 2004; R. E. Smith & Smoll, 2002; Thompson, 2003). Rather, winning should be viewed as a consequence of performers' physical and psychological development and not as the primary focus of athletic involvement (Cumming, Smoll, Smith, & Grossbard, 2007). This is particularly emphasized relative to youth sport. Herein lies the separation of philosophies. It is likely that the importance of winning and losing increases with age and/or level of competition. A developmental model of sport, with an emphasis on giving maximum effort, working to develop one's skills, and enjoying the social and competitive aspects of the sport experience, rather than the only objective being to beat one's opponent, is advocated for youth sport (Cumming et al., 2007; Martens, 2004; Smoll & Smith, 2005). This environment should increase the likelihood of athletes realizing their potential for personal growth. Moreover, the prevalence of fear of failure in achievement settings, and its negative effects on psychological and physical well-being, represents an important social concern (Conroy, 2001). Over-emphasizing competition in the early phases of training will always cause shortcomings in athletic abilities later in performers' careers (Balyi & Hamilton, 2003). Sport represents one of the most significant achievement domains for children, and the emphasis ought to be on reducing fear of failure in young athletes and helping them with both performance-related factors and their social development (Saferstein, 2005, 2006).

However, as the competitive level gets higher, there must be a concomitant rise in an additional attribute. For performers to be successful in the win- and profit-oriented environment that characterizes professional sport, they must develop and nurture a "winning mentality". Possession of this mentality is particularly crucial when "even when less than his best, the champion is better than his opponent at winning" (Barnes, 2008e, p. 71). To be the best, you must think you are the best. To win, you have to believe you will win. I hasten to stress that this winning mentality is in conjunction with, and does not replace, the developmental model attributes mentioned previously. Winning isn't everything, but its proportionate emphasis increases with level of competition.

Winning has been found to result in "a range of pleasant emotional outcomes and reductions in arousal and stress" (G. V. Wilson & Kerr, 1999, p. 85). On the other hand, the same study reported that losing produces unpleasant emotional reactions and reduced arousal. In particular, athletes have reported significantly higher levels of anxiety, humiliation, and sullenness following losses compared with after victories (Kerr, Wilson, Bowling, & Sheahan, 2005). Winning feels good. Victory serves to refresh the conquerors' endeavours and, many would say, justifies the means. Losing is painful. Defeated athletes often suffer an according collapse of will. However, an erroneous display of mental toughness is to project oneself as a bad loser. A bad loser is not the same as a mentally tough athlete. Mental toughness is being gracious in defeat and retiring respectfully to the sidelines to give the victors their deserved limelight. Though beaten, the mentally tough athlete may, for example, hold on to the "proud memory of courage and unyielding commitment shown in the face of overwhelming force" (A. O'Connor, 2003, p. 39). Such an athlete possesses the courage to endure the misery of defeat. Similarly, the victorious athlete is decorous and honourable so as not to bask in the despair of a downed opponent. The victory should be enjoyed, but there ought to be no place for triumphalism in the heart of the mentally tough performer.

Ever-higher levels of excellence are not achieved with self-congratulation. Greatness has never recognized coasting. The pursuit of the next horizon is a characteristic of the mentally tough performer. As the most successful soccer manager in the history of the British game, Manchester United's Sir Alex Ferguson, put it after a victory which put his team ahead in the league championship and on course for their record-equalling 18th title: "It's time to kick on" (as cited in Syed, 2009b, p. 71). Unerring focus.

The philosopher A. C. Grayling sums it up perfectly: "It is what we aspire to be that colours our characters – and it is our trying, not just our succeeding, which ennobles them" (Grayling, 2001, p. 25). For the athlete, there are lessons to be learnt from suffering defeat. Very often, the best ones are also the hardest; and defeat counts among these. Being a bad loser is just that – a bad loser. As Franz Beckenbauer, Germany's most revered footballer, said: "Defeat belongs to life like victory" (as cited in Cameron, 1995, p. 112). Similarly, having won the final race of the season but, ultimately, missing out on the 2008 Formula One drivers' championship by a single point, Felipe Massa was gracious in defeat: "I know how to win and I know how to lose. It is one more day of my life and we are going to learn a lot from this" (as cited in Gorman, 2008b, p. 76). The gratitude, humility, and sportsmanship demonstrated by American golfer Kenny Perry having just lost the 2009 US Masters play-off had the attending media spellbound by such benevolence we too seldom witness (Reason, 2009b). To act like this requires the courage that, along with the other personality attributes identified in this chapter, is constitutive of mental toughness. A final word on winning and losing: the mentally tough performer is not dedicated to the philosophy of winning at all costs. As Simon Barnes of *The Times* quite rightly observed at the time of a particularly nasty Test cricket series between Australia and India that dripped with mutual enmity, "the way you win matters just as much" (Barnes, 2008d, p. 66).

A championship mindset

Finally in this chapter, I wish to begin the process of conceptualizing mental toughness (Chapters 2 and 3 take this much further). Several years ago I received a letter from Professor Allan Snyder of the Centre for the Mind at the University of Sydney. He was intrigued by a report he had read in the *New Scientist* (Young, 2001). In it, I stated that psychological superiority alone could explain why Australia had won six consecutive Rugby League World Cup tournaments between 1975 and 2000. Since previous research into rugby league football has not identified significant differences in physical and tactical preparation (Brewer & Davis, 1995), I argued it seems that, regardless of physical attributes, the tougher athlete often prevails, and the difference between success and failure is often more easily, and perhaps more appropriately, attributable to psychological factors. This struck a chord. In accordance with my own view, Snyder had stated in a publication at the time: "Two athletes may enter a race with similar bodies, even similar training, but their mindset will be different" (Snyder, 1999, p. 71). He added: "It is our mindset that ultimately limits our expectations of ourselves and which circumscribes our boundaries. It is our mindset which determines whether or not we have the courage to challenge others and to expand our horizons" (p. 73). My view is that mental toughness should be conceptualized as a personality style and mindset, shaped by experiences, culture, society, training, and, quite possibly, genetics. Snyder believes that it is, and that "the world is viewed in its totality through this mindset" (p. 73). Moreover, he advocates that such a mindset "is the transferable commodity, not the skill itself" (p. 73).

Psychologist Carol Dweck has suggested that the mindset distinguishes great athletes (i.e., the champions) from others. Without denying the importance of an individual's talent, we ought to look more closely at the commitment, discipline, and perseverance that go into success. Of Jackie Joyner-Kersee, Mia Hamm, and Muhammad Ali, Dweck (2006) observed that, yes, they had talent; but they also had the right mindset. Perhaps one of the best definitions of mental toughness comes from former Green Bay Packers football coach and NFL Hall of Famer, Vince Lombardi. In the early 1960s, Lombardi transformed the Packers from perennial losers to winners. He was known as a person who demanded excellence and never accepted mediocrity. He said: "Mental toughness is many things and rather difficult to explain. Its qualities are sacrifice and self-denial. Also, most importantly, it is combined with a perfectly disciplined will that refuses to give in. It's a state of mind – you could call it character in action" (as cited in Curtis Management Group, 1998, p. 20). I agree with Lombardi, Dweck, and Snyder. A world of opportunities exists. The saddest words in the English language are "could have . . . might have . . . should have . . . would have . . . didn't." Mental toughness affords great minds to think big. If you believe you can do it, you probably can.

This introductory chapter discussed the characteristics purportedly constitutive of mental toughness as reported by the popular media. Further, consideration was given to the moderating role of mental toughness in guiding athletes to consider appropriate reactions to win–loss outcomes. As a conclusion to this introduction, I would like to give the last words to two sporting greats. United States swimming legend Michael Phelps (dual record holder of most Olympic gold medals, and most won at a single Games) stated of the "mental" contribution to his success: "Our mental outlook is one of the few things that we can truly control. Training we must view as a privilege, and act accordingly. We must first look inward to find solutions to challenges. The solution lies with us" (as cited in Lord, 2007, p. 70). Seven-times winner of the Tour de France, American cyclist Lance Armstrong epitomizes mental toughness. After suffering from cancer, most competitors would be thankful that they were alive. Instead, Armstrong returned to competitive cycling to accomplish the seemingly impossible. Interviewed after his fifth triumph, he reflected: "When you feel like giving up, you have to ask yourself which you would rather live with. What the Tour de France teaches you is that pain is temporary, quitting is forever" (as cited in Philip, 2004, p. S5). These defining qualities truly reflect a mentally tough and championship mindset.

2 Characterizing mental toughness

Nothing that is of real worth can be achieved without courageous
working.

Samuel Smiles

Introduction

Mental toughness has often been associated with peak sport performance, particularly in popular sporting discourse (see Chapter
1) as a synonym for determination or resilience (Moran, 2004). As
mentioned also in the previous chapter, top sportspeople have
frequently cited mental toughness as the crucial prerequisite of
sporting success (e.g., Gould et al., 1987, 2002). Moreover,
research findings have emphasized the importance of mental
toughness in developing champion sport performers (e.g., Durand-
Bush & Salmela, 2002; Norris, 1999).

The term has also been used as a euphemism for sport
psychology in relabelling efforts to sell the benefits of the latter to
English soccer players and their coaches (Pain & Harwood, 2004).
Virtually any positive and desirable psychological characteristic
associated with success has been, at some time, labelled as mental
toughness. However, perhaps due to its seemingly amorphous
structure, the term "mental toughness" is seldom found in academic psychology. Indeed, it is a new topic requiring exploration
relative to the psychology of sporting excellence (Gould, 2002).
Though the term is intuitively appealing and used equally gener-
ously by players, coaches, and the sport media, an adequate

definition has been elusive (Cashmore, 2002; Clough, Earle, & Sewell, 2002). Several definitions have been proffered to address this lack of conceptual clarity, including an ability to cope with stress and pressure (e.g., Goldberg, 1998), to rebound from failures (e.g., Woods, Hocton, & Desmond, 1995), and to show resilience (e.g., Tutko & Richards, 1976). However, research on stress, resilience, and vulnerability in sport has been characterized by definitional circularity. Mental toughness, in particular, has suffered from a general lack of conceptual clarity. Indeed, the construct has been criticized as being "rather nebulous" (Moran, 2004, p. 10). Therefore, a theoretical model of the construct of mental toughness would provide terminological refinement on the vulnerability–resilience continuum and address this criticism.

While athletes and coaches often talk about mental toughness, seldom has it been precisely defined. This is in spite of the literature including numerous contributions dedicated to the notion of developing mentally tough sport performers. In this chapter, the attempts of the extant literature to gain a consensual definition of mental toughness, and its constitutive characteristics, are presented.

In search of mental toughness

Fons et origo

As part of his pioneering sport psychology work, Coleman Griffith (1926, 1928) examined the personality profiles of successful athletes. Through observations of and interviews with university and professional athletes, Griffith identified 11 characteristics attributable to their success (see Table 2.1). Many sport performers since have completed many more personality inventories. Interestingly, Griffith's inter-war characteristics and those elicited from the first sport-specific personality inventory, Tutko and co-workers' Athletic Motivation Inventory (AMI; Tutko, Lyon, & Ogilvie, 1969), more than 40 years later, reveal a striking commonality (Table 2.1). Particularly noteworthy is the AMI's ninth characteristic – mental toughness.

Table 2.1 Personality characteristics associated with superior athletes

Griffith (1926)	Tutko et al. (1969)
Ruggedness	Drive
Courage	Determination
Intelligence	Leadership
Exuberance	Aggressiveness
Buoyance	Guilt proneness
Emotional adjustment	Emotional control
Optimism	Self-confidence
Conscientiousness	Conscientiousness
Alertness	Mental toughness
Loyalty	Trust
Respect for authority	Coachability

The quest for a definition

Mental toughness is a bit like "talent" or "charisma": instinctively recognizable, but endlessly tricky to pin down in a definition. The earliest attempts to define mental toughness proposed that it was a personality trait (Cattell, Blewett, & Beloff, 1955; Kroll, 1967; Werner & Gottheil, 1966). Considered as "tough-mindedness", and manifested in realistic, self-reliant, and cynical behaviour, this trait was one of 16 that described personality (Cattell, 1957). Interestingly, mental toughness has also been viewed as a state of mind (Gibson, 1998). Subsequent contributions have attempted to elucidate the term; however, the literature has struggled to arrive at a definitional consensus. Research has provided such varied definitions as: an ability to cope with pressure, stress, and adversity (e.g., Bull, Shambrook, James, & Brooks, 2005; Clough et al., 2002; Fourie & Potgieter, 2001; Gould et al., 1987; G. Jones, Hanton, & Connaughton, 2002; Middleton, Marsh, Martin, Richards, & Perry, 2004a; R. E. Smith & Smoll, 1989; Thelwell, Weston, & Greenlees, 2005; R. M. Williams, 1988); an ability to overcome or rebound from setbacks (e.g., Dennis, 1981; Gould et al., 1987; G. Jones et al., 2002; Loehr, 1995; Taylor, 1989; Tutko & Richards, 1976); an ability to persist or a refusal to quit (e.g., Cashmore, 2002; Dennis, 1981; Fourie & Potgieter, 2001; Goldberg, 1998; Gould et al., 1987; G. Jones et al., 2002; Loehr, 1995); an ability to withstand strong criticism and to avoid becoming upset when losing or performing poorly (e.g., Clough et al., 2002; Loehr, 1995; Tutko & Richards, 1972); an insensitivity or resilience (e.g., Alderman, 1974; Clough et al., 2002; Goldberg, 1998; Loehr, 1995); an ability to maintain an optimal mindset throughout a sporting event (e.g., Cashmore, 2002; J. W. Jones, Neuman, Altmann, & Dreschler, 2001); a willingness to take personal responsibility (e.g., Bull et al., 2005; Fourie & Potgieter, 2001); an ability to show dedication and commitment (e.g., Bull et al., 2005; Fourie & Potgieter, 2001); an ability to believe in self (e.g., Bull et al., 2005; Clough et al., 2002; Thelwell et al., 2005); qualities of mind or intellect (e.g., Cashmore, 2005); and the possession of superior mental skills (e.g., Bull, Albinson, & Shambrook, 1996; Fourie & Potgieter, 2001; Golby & Sheard, 2004; Golby, Sheard, & Lavallee, 2003; Loehr, 1986, 1995).

Characteristics of mentally tough performers

Similarly, the proposed characteristics of mentally tough performers in the extant literature have been wide ranging. Examples include: confidence, optimism, self-belief, and self-esteem (e.g., Bull et al., 1996, 2005; Cashmore, 2002; Favret & Benzel, 1997; Fourie & Potgieter, 2001; Goldberg, 1998; Gould et al., 1987; Graham & Yocom, 1990; Hodge, 1994; G. Jones et al., 2002; Loehr, 1986, 1995; Luszki, 1982; Pankey, 1993; Taylor, 1989; Thelwell et al., 2005; Woods ct al., 1995); achieving consistency (e.g., Clough et al., 2002; Fourie & Potgieter, 2001; Gould et al., 1987; Graham & Yocom, 1990; Loehr, 1986; R. M. Williams, 1988); commitment, desire, and determination (e.g., Bull et al., 1996, 2005; Cashmore, 2002; Clough et al., 2002; Fourie & Potgieter, 2001; Goldberg, 1998; Hodge, 1994; G. Jones et al., 2002; Loehr, 1986; Luszki, 1982; Middleton et al., 2004a; Thelwell et al., 2005; Tunney, 1987; R. M. Williams, 1988); concentration and focus (e.g., Cashmore, 2002; Fourie & Potgieter, 2001; Goldberg, 1998; Graham & Yocom, 1990; C. M. Jones, 1982; G. Jones et al., 2002; Loehr, 1986; Luszki, 1982; Middleton et al., 2004a; Thelwell et al., 2005; Tunney, 1987); and control, courage, motivation, and willpower (e.g., Bull et al., 1996; Cashmore, 2002; Favret & Benzel, 1997; Gould et al., 1987; Graham & Yocom, 1990; Hodge, 1994; G. Jones et al., 2002; Loehr,

1986; Thelwell et al., 2005; Tunney, 1987; Tutko & Richards, 1976; Woods et al., 1995).

Interestingly, American coach and educationalist Harvey Dorfman prefers to use the term *mental discipline* rather than *mental toughness*. Whatever the preferred term, he refers to the aspects of mental toughness as disciplines of one's mind; namely, courage, intensity, competitiveness, consistency of focus, a confrontational attitude, aggressiveness under control, relentlessness, responsibility to do what the situation requires, responsibility for one's own behaviour, honesty, self-sacrifice, self-trust, an ability to make necessary adjustments, an ability to compete with pain, a positive approach to task and circumstance, an ability to cope effectively with adversity, an indifference to an opponent's presence or posturing, and an ability to do always what needs to be done (Dorfman, 2003). Somewhat modestly, he admits that these aspects may not be all inclusive of mental toughness. However, I would suggest that they go some way to characterizing a particular state of mind; that is, a mentally tough mindset. Conceptual refinement of the aspects may be required; however, as Dorfman (p. 167) states: "An athlete who checks off all of the above as being representative of his own makeup qualifies as a mentally tough individual."

Recent qualitative developments

Given the aforementioned diverse range of characteristics, it is perhaps unsurprising that efforts to provide a narrow definition have, arguably, contributed to mental toughness being one of the least understood terms in sport psychology. Rather than criticizing the construct for its historical propensity to be defined in diverse ways, research should be directed toward categorizing those characteristics required to be a mentally tough performer. Despite the apparent breadth of opinion, there appears to be broad agreement on the requisite attributes of mentally tough performers. However, recent qualitative research on the issue of mental toughness has still concerned itself with defining the construct and determining the essential attributes required to be a mentally tough performer.

For example, Sansonette Fourie and Justus Potgieter investigated the components of mental toughness as reported in written statements by 131 expert coaches and 160 elite-level sport performers recruited from 31 different sports (Fourie & Potgieter, 2001). Data responses from the coaches ($n = 534$) and from the athletes ($n = 488$) were content analysed through a consensual procedure. Inductive content analysis resulted in 41 higher-order themes that were summarized into 12 mental toughness umbrella categories; namely, motivational level, coping skills, confidence maintenance, cognitive skill, discipline and goal-directedness, competitiveness, possession of prerequisite physical and mental requirements, team unity, preparation skills, psychological hardiness, religious convictions, and ethics.

In another qualitative investigation of mental toughness, Graham Jones and co-workers asked 10 international sportspeople to (a) define mental toughness, and (b) identify and describe their perception of the attributes of the ideal mentally tough performer (G. Jones et al., 2002). Subsequently, the interviewees were asked to place these attributes in rank order of importance. Twelve attributes were identified from the first question (see Table 2.2).

The athletes defined the construct of mental toughness as the cognitive and behavioural efforts of a performer to have superior self-regulatory skills (G. Jones et al., 2002). Their perception of the mentally tough performer was someone who is able, generally, to cope better than opponents with the many competition, training, and lifestyle demands that sport places on him/her. Of equal interest was the assessment of how a performer, specifically, is more consistent and better than opponents in remaining determined, focused, confident, and in control under pressure. Using similar investigative techniques to their 2002 study, the same authors verified their earlier definition of mental toughness in a follow-up study (G. Jones, Hanton, & Connaughton, 2007). "Super-elite" sport performers (i.e., Olympic or World Champions), coaches, and sport psychologists categorized 30 attributes under 13 subcomponents that were essential to being mentally tough. These attributes (see Table 2.3) were clustered under four separate dimensions (namely, attitude/mindset, training, competition, and postcompetition) within an overall framework of mental toughness.

The attitude/mindset dimension was divided into two subcomponents (belief and focus), which enabled mentally tough

Table 2.2 Mental toughness attributes and importance ranking

Overall rank	Attribute
1	Having an unshakeable self-belief in your ability to achieve your competition goals
2	Bouncing back from performance setbacks as a result of increased determination to succeed
3	Having an unshakeable self-belief that you possess unique qualities and abilities that make you better than your opponents
=4	Having an insatiable desire and internalized motives to succeed
=4	Remaining fully focused on the task at hand in the face of competition-specific distractions
6	Regaining psychological control following unexpected, uncontrollable events (competition-specific)
7	Pushing back the boundaries of physical and emotional pain, while still maintaining technique and effort under distress (in training and competition)
8	Accepting that competition anxiety is inevitable and knowing that you can cope with it
=9	Thriving on the pressure of competition
=9	Not being adversely affected by others' good and bad performances
11	Remaining fully focused in the face of personal life distractions
12	Switching a sport focus on and off as required

Source: Adapted from G. Jones et al. (2002).

performers to remain on course in achieving their ultimate goal, irrespective of obstacles and circumstances. The training dimension reflected how mentally tough performers were able to keep motivation levels high, and used every aspect of the training environment and challenging situation to their advantage when dealing with years of patience, discipline, and work required to reach the highest standards. The third dimension, competition, explained how the ideal mentally tough performer behaved under the extreme pressure of high-level competitions. Post-competition, the final dimension, contained two sub-components that described the rationalization of competition failures and successes (G. Jones et al., 2007).

Focusing on professional soccer, Richard Thelwell and co-workers aimed to confirm the findings of the G. Jones et al. (2002)

Table 2.3 G. Jones et al.'s (2007) mental toughness framework

Dimension	Sub-category	Rank and description
Attitude/ mindset	Belief	1 Having an unshakeable self-belief as a result of total awareness of how you got to where you are now.
		2 Having an inner arrogance that makes you believe that you can achieve anything you set your mind to.
		3 Having the belief that you can punch through any obstacle people put in your way.
		4 Believing that your desire or hunger will ultimately result in your fulfilling your potential.
	Focus	5 Refusing to be swayed by short-term gains (financial, performance) that will jeopardize the achievement of long-term goals.
		6 Ensuring that achievement of your sport's goal is the number-one priority in your life.
		7 Recognizing the importance of knowing when to switch on and off from your sport.
Training	Using long-term goals as the source of motivation	1 When training gets tough (physically and mentally) because things are not going your way, keeping yourself going by reminding yourself of your goals and aspirations and why you're putting yourself through it.
		2 Having the patience, discipline, and self-control with the required training for each specific developmental stage to allow you to reach your full potential.
	Controlling the environment	3 Remaining in control and not controlled.
		=4 Using all aspects of a very difficult training environment to your advantage.
	Pushing yourself to the limit	=4 Loving the bits of training that hurt.
		6 Thriving on opportunities to beat other people in training.
Competition	Handling pressure	1 Loving the pressure of competition.
		3 Adapting to and coping with any change/distraction/threat under pressure.

(continues)

Table 2.3 (*continued*)

Dimension	Sub-category	Rank and description
		5 Making the correct decisions and choosing the right options that secure optimal performance under conditions of extreme pressure and ambiguity.
		8 Coping with and channelling anxiety in pressure situations.
	Belief	2 Total commitment to your performance goal until every possible opportunity of success has passed.
		4 Not being fazed by making mistakes and then coming back from them.
	Regulating performance	6 Having a killer instinct to capitalize on the moment when you know you can win.
		7 Raising your performance "up a gear" when it matters most.
	Staying focused	9 Totally focusing on the job at hand in the face of distraction.
		11 Remaining committed to a self-absorbed focus despite external distractions.
		=12 In certain performances, remaining focused on processes and not solely outcomes.
	Awareness and control of thoughts and feelings	10 Being acutely aware of any inappropriate thoughts and feelings and changing them to help perform optimally.
	Controlling the environment	=12 Using all aspects of a very difficult competition environment to your advantage.
Post-competition	Handling failure	1 Recognizing and rationalizing failure and picking out the learning points to take forward.
		2 Using failure to drive yourself to further success.
	Handling success	3 Knowing when to celebrate success and then stop and focus on the next challenge.
		4 Knowing how to rationally handle success.

Source: Adapted from G. Jones et al. (2007).

study (Thelwell et al., 2005). The main aim of their study was to examine further the definition and attributes of mental toughness within a specific soccer population. The authors' approach was to counter the effect of inter-sport variations, which they suggested had arisen from research attempts to identify mental toughness characteristics from a general, rather than specific, sport perspective. These authors reported two studies, with interviews from the first suggesting a general consensus with the Jones et al. definition. The sole variation was the finding that mentally tough soccer players should always (as opposed to "generally") cope better than their opponents with the demands of the sport. There were also slight variances with regard to the attributes deemed essential for mental toughness, which may be attributable to the specificity of the sport.

Despite 10 qualities being identified, not all participants mentioned each of them. Key mental toughness characteristics were perceived as more important than others. Specifically, all six participants mentioned that having the total self-belief at all times that one will achieve, having the ability to react to situations positively, having the ability to hang on and be calm under pressure, and having the ability to ignore distractions and remain focused, were critical to the mentally tough performer. Five participants identified that wanting the ball at all times (when playing well and not so well), knowing what it takes to grind oneself out of trouble, and controlling emotions through performance, were vital qualities. Four participants commented on the importance of having a presence that affects opponents, and having everything in control outside of the game, while three commented on the need to enjoy the pressure associated with performance (Thelwell et al., 2005).

Other researchers, however, asserted that the G. Jones et al. (2002) study was inadequate as it only described the outcomes of being mentally tough and did not define mental toughness itself (Middleton et al., 2004a). Employing a qualitative grounded theory approach following semi-structured interviews, Cory Middleton and colleagues defined mental toughness as "an unshakeable perseverance and conviction towards some goal despite pressure or adversity" (Middleton et al.). These authors also identified 12 key mental toughness characteristics; namely, *self-efficacy* in one's ability to achieve in a chosen sport, belief in one's own *potential* and capacity for growth and development, a strong and positive *mental self-concept* with regard to dealing with adversity, *task familiarity* and understanding adversity, *task value* in the quality and success of performance, intrinsic motivation to achieve *personal bests*, intellectual and emotional *goal commitment*, *perseverance* in the face of adversity, *task-specific attention* whilst being able to block out distracting or negative thoughts, *positivity* when faced with adversity, *stress minimization* when under pressure or adversity, and *positive comparisons* with one's opponents in coping better with adversity.

Importantly, Middleton et al. (2004a) used existing theory that had parallels with the emergent mental toughness characteristics (i.e., self-concept theory, attentional styles, self-determination theory) in order to develop a preliminary conceptual model. This model was both multidimensional and hierarchical, attempting to capture the complexity of mental toughness with greater specificity, and separating mental toughness into orientation and strategy. The authors argued that their definition and model not only illustrates what mental toughness is, but also describes the actions of mental toughness (e.g., perseverance, task focus, emotion management), coupled with the personality characteristics that orientate people to be mentally tough (e.g., self-belief, motivation, commitment).

Similar actions and personality characteristics emerged from two recent qualitative single-sport investigations of mental toughness. Interviews with elite English cricketers yielded five mental toughness general dimensions; namely, developmental factors, personal responsibility, dedication and commitment, belief, and coping with pressure (Bull et al., 2005). Of particular interest, analysis of the focused interview transcripts identified the critical role of the players' environments in influencing tough character, tough attitudes, and tough thinking, and how these manifest in players' actions. A study of experienced Australian Rules football coaches identified and ranked 11 characteristics; namely, self-belief, work ethic, personal values, self-motivated, tough attitude, concentration and focus, resilience, handling pressure, emotional intelligence, sport intelligence, and physical toughness (Gucciardi, Gordon, & Dimmock, 2008). The study's authors proposed that mental toughness is "a quality that brings together several human features and allows a footballer to consistently get the best out of his physical ability" (p. 278). Their findings also identified those situations that demand mental toughness and the behaviours commonly displayed by mentally tough Australian Rules footballers. Specific to Australian Football, Gucciardi et al. determined that mental toughness "is a collection of values, attitudes, behaviours, and emotions that enable you to persevere and overcome any obstacle, adversity, or pressure experienced, but also to maintain concentration and motivation when things are going well to consistently achieve your goals" (p. 278).

An emerging consensus

A summarized overview of the aforementioned qualitative studies is presented in Table 2.4. A consistent picture has appeared from the recent spate of qualitative studies and a consensus has emerged of what is constitutive of mental toughness. My criticism levelled at much of the qualitative research presented in this chapter is that it has contributed little to furthering our understanding of mental toughness. As we shall see, it can be argued that a comparison of these recent qualitative findings with what was already known yields substantial similarities. It is also apparent that the G. Jones et al. (2002) study is often cited by other researchers of mental toughness seeking confirmation of the validity of their own qualitative findings (e.g., Lane, Thelwell, & Gill, 2007; Thelwell et al., 2005). Given the overlap between the rationales and methods of the G. Jones et al. (2002, 2007) studies, it is worth taking a closer look at participants' responses. The definitions elicited from volunteers in these studies highlight the multivariate nature of the mental toughness construct and assume the necessity of aggregating such psychological skills into meaningful mental toughness attributes. Moreover, when the participants were invited to elaborate on their answers, it is apparent that their perception of the attributes of the ideal mentally tough performer reflects those of athletes many years earlier (see Tables 2.5 and 2.6).

Table 2.4 Summary of key published studies investigating mental toughness

Study	Method	Data obtained	Participants	Sports represented	N	Findings	Limitations
Fourie and Potgieter (2001)	Written statements	Qualitative	Expert coaches (mean age = 42.7 years; range = 22–85) who had an average of 14.3 years' coaching experience Elite-level sport performers (mean age = 21 years; range = 14–35) competing at international, national, provincial, or 1st-team university level	31 sport codes (unspecified by authors)	131 coaches (93 males, 38 females) 160 sport performers (87 males, 73 females)	The identification of 12 components of mental toughness Coaches and sport performers differed in their opinion as to the most important characteristics	The coaches and sport performers were quite varied in their description of the characteristics of mental toughness Fails to relate findings to extant mental toughness research literature, especially Loehr's work
Clough et al. (2002)	Questionnaires	Qualitative/ quantitative	Sport performers (no further demographic data available)	A range of sports (unspecified by authors)	>600 (males and females)	The design and development of an instrument to measure mental toughness (MT48)	Much additional validation evidence is required before the MT48 can be accepted as a worthwhile tool for the measurement of mental toughness

(continues)

Table 2.4 (continued)

Study	Method	Data obtained	Participants	Sports represented	N	Findings	Limitations
G. Jones et al. (2002)	Individual interviews and focus groups	Qualitative	International sport performers (mean age = 31.2 years; SD = 5.3) who had achieved full international honours and represented their country in major events (e.g., Olympic/Commonwealth Games) and had an average of 5 years' international experience	Swimming, sprinting, artistic and rhythmic gymnastics, trampoline, middle-distance running, triathlon, golf, rugby union, and netball	10 (7 males, 3 females)	A definition of mental toughness and 12 attributes of the ideal mentally tough performer emerged. The resulting definition emphasized both general and specific dimensions	Range and number of sports sampled. Small sample size. Using only one focus group with three individuals
Middleton et al. (2004a)	Individual interviews	Qualitative	Elite sport performers (mean age = 37.7 years; SD = 13.4; range = 25–70)	Track and field, swimming, boxing, hockey, rowing, archery, basketball, mountain running, marathon, climbing, rugby union, rugby league, Australian Rules football, baseball, cricket, cycling, water	33 (21 males, 12 females) of whom 25 were sport performers, and 8 were non-athletes	The identification of 12 mental toughness characteristics	Conclusion that mental toughness exists only in relation to overcoming adversity The relative contribution of each of the 12

Study	Method	Participants	Sport	N	Findings	Limitations
			polo, squash, netball, triathlon, power lifting, and physically disabled track and field			characteristics has not yet been established
Thelwell et al. (2005)	Individual interviews	Qualitative	Professional soccer players (mean age = 28.8 years; $SD = 4.8$), all with international playing experience	Soccer	6 (all males)	A definition of mental toughness and 10 qualities were identified (though not all participants mentioned each of them)	Very small sample size. Only one sport represented. Focus group rather than individual interviews may have been more appropriate
Bull et al. (2005)	Individual interviews	Qualitative	Professional cricketers (nominated by coaches for their "mental toughness") who had represented England in international Test and one-day competition	Cricket	12 (all males)	The identification of 5 general dimensions within 4 structural categories	Only one sport represented

(*continues*)

Table 2.4 (continued)

Study	Method	Data obtained	Participants	Sports represented	N	Findings	Limitations
G. Jones et al. (2007)	Focus groups and individual interviews	Qualitative	Olympic or world champion sport performers (age range = 25–48 years) who had an average of 6 years of experience at this "super-elite" level and who had won at least one gold medal at an Olympic Games or world championship Coaches (age range = 38–60 years) and sport psychologists (age range = 35–45 years) who had coached or consulted with Olympic or world champions on a long-term basis	Boxing, swimming, athletics, judo, triathlon, rowing, pentathlon, squash, cricket, and rugby union	8 sport performers (5 males, 3 females) 3 coaches (all males), 4 sport psychologists (all males)	The identification of 30 attributes clustered under 4 separate dimensions	Omission of coaches and sport psychologists in the focus group

Gucciardi et al. (2008)	Individual interviews	Qualitative	Coaches (mean age = 42 years; SD = 9.6), all with considerable elite-level playing and coaching experience	Australian Rules football	11 coaches (all males)	The identification of 11 key characteristics within 3 independent categories	Use of self-report data. Reliance on elite-level volunteers only

Table 2.5 The commonality of attributes identified by G. Jones et al. (2002) and Loehr's (1986) previously identified mental toughness subscales

G. Jones et al. mental toughness attributes	Examples of participant quotes from G. Jones et al. (pp. 210–213)	Loehr subscales
Having an unshakeable self-belief in your ability to achieve your competition goals	"Mental toughness is about your self-belief and not being shaken from your path . . . it is producing the goods and having the self-belief in your head to produce the goods."	Self-confidence
Bouncing back from performance setbacks as a result of increased determination to succeed	"Nobody's rise to the top is completely smooth, there are always little hiccups or turns in the road."	Attitude control
Having an unshakeable self-belief that you possess unique qualities and abilities that make you better than your opponents	"He had the self-belief in his ability to know he was making the right decisions."	Self-confidence
Having an insatiable desire and internalized motives to succeed	"You've really got to want it, but you've also got to want to do it for yourself. You've also got to really understand why you're in it."	Motivation
Remaining fully focused on the task at hand in the face of competition-specific distractions	"If you want to be the best, you have got to be totally focused on what you are doing. There are inevitable distractions and you just have to be able to focus on what you need to focus on."	Attention control

Regaining psychological control following unexpected, uncontrollable events (competition-specific)	"It's definitely about not getting unsettled by things you didn't expect or can't control. You've got to be able to switch back into control mode."	Negative energy control Attention control
Pushing back the boundaries of physical and emotional pain, while still maintaining technique and effort under distress (in training and competition)	"In my sport you have to deal with the physical pain from fatigue, dehydration, and tiredness . . . you are depleting your body of so many different things. It is a question of pushing yourself . . . it's mind over matter, just trying to hold your technique and perform while under this distress and go beyond your limits."	Motivation Attitude control
Accepting that competition anxiety is inevitable and knowing that you can cope with it	"I accept that I'm going to get nervous, particularly when the pressure's on, but keeping the lid on it and being in control is crucial."	Negative energy control
Thriving on the pressure of competition	"If you are going to achieve anything worthwhile, there is bound to be pressure. Mental toughness is being resilient to and using the competition pressure to get the best out of yourself."	Positive energy
Not being adversely affected by others' good and bad performances	"The mentally tough performer uses others' good performances as a spur."	Motivation
Remaining fully focused in the face of personal life distractions	"Once you're in the competition, you cannot let your mind wander to other things. It doesn't matter what has happened to you, you can't bring the problem into the performance arena."	Attention control
Switching a sport focus on and off as required	"The mentally tough performer succeeds by having control of the on/off switch."	Attention control

Source: Adapted from G. Jones et al. (2002) and Loehr (1986).

Table 2.6 The commonality of descriptions identified by G. Jones et al. (2007) and Loehr's (1986) previously identified mental toughness subscales

G. Jones et al. mental toughness descriptions [sub-category]	Examples of participant quotes from G. Jones et al. (pp. 248–260)	Loehr subscales
Having an inner arrogance that makes you believe that you can achieve anything you set your mind to [Belief]	"It's that inner arrogance, that bit of an attitude towards things that I set my mind to. It is never ever giving up and knowing that if I just persevere I know that I am going to be able to do it. . . . I believe I will be able to do it."	Self-confidence
Refusing to be swayed by short-term gains (financial, performance) that will jeopardize the achievement of long-term goals [Focus]	"The mentally tough performer will not be swayed by short-term goals, such as money or minor successes, in their desire to achieve their ultimate goal. You can think of many athletes who turn down vast amounts of money that are offered by promoters or sponsors to run in marathons . . . or compete or play in competitions . . . or go on tours, so that they can focus on their long-term goal . . . you know . . . the Olympics or Worlds."	Motivation
When training gets tough (physically and mentally) because things are not going your way, keeping yourself going by reminding yourself of your goals and aspirations and why you're putting yourself through it [Using long-term goals as the source of motivation]	"Life gets difficult, training gets difficult, but the mentally tough athletes know exactly why they are doing it . . . They know what their goals and aspirations are and why they are putting themselves through the hard work." "I am doing this because I want to win gold. . . . Mentally tough performers acknowledge that they are tired but realize and remind themselves that if they are to achieve their goal they have to get back in the gym and work."	Motivation Attitude control

Using all aspects of a very difficult training environment to your advantage [Controlling the environment]	"At training camps you don't always get things your way. . . . You've got to be able to train with other people in the training environment there. It may not be ideal for you but you've got to deal with that and use it to your advantage. The mentally tough performer can handle the environment he is put in and use it to his advantage."	Negative energy control Attitude control
Thriving on opportunities to beat other people in training [Pushing yourself to the limit]	"Their identity is caught up with . . . 'I am very good, I am going to prove it, I am going to take you out of this and beat you.' . . . They thrive on opportunities of beating other people and are not afraid to put themselves on the line."	Self-confidence Attitude control
Making the correct decisions and choosing the right options that secure optimal performance under conditions of extreme pressure and ambiguity [Handling pressure]	"Sometimes it is about curbing your initial instincts in a pressure situation, because the instinct says 'go for it now,' whereas, actually, the best option might be to wait 5 minutes before you go for it. Mentally tough performers are able to make the right decisions . . . and know when that is. . . . They will make the right decision when it is required."	Attention control
Not being fazed by making mistakes and then coming back from them [Belief]	"Mistakes would get some people down because they start worrying and thinking about failure. The ideal mentally tough performer can put a mistake to one side and carry on performing regardless. They have a resilience, a toughness, they are not fazed by mistakes. They stay mentally strong when things do go wrong, they are able to bounce back from mistakes or errors . . . and then produce it again."	Negative energy control Positive energy Attitude control

(continues)

Table 2.6 (continued)

G. Jones et al. mental toughness descriptions [sub-category]	Examples of participant quotes from G. Jones et al. (pp. 248–260)	Loehr subscales
Raising your performance "up a gear" when it matters most [Regulating performance]	"If somebody in a heat breaks the world record, you know you are going to have to do the same. In a final you might have to break the world record to win, you have to be prepared to break the world record to win, and the mentally tough performer can and, importantly, knows how to do that."	Self-confidence Positive energy
Remaining committed to a self-absorbed focus despite external distractions [Staying focused]	"They are in a cocoon almost, absorbed in themselves, committed to what they're doing, what they need to do, how they're going to react. Regardless of what happens, mentally tough performers remain committed to what they should be focused on, despite the efforts of other people and circumstances that try to draw them out of it."	Attention control
Being acutely aware of any inappropriate thoughts and feelings and changing them to help perform optimally [Awareness and control of thoughts and feelings]	"They have this recognition mechanism that kicks in, but the key difference between them and other athletes is that the mentally tough ones are able to change that thought or feeling so that they can perform at their best."	Negative energy control Attitude control
Using all aspects of a very difficult competition environment to your advantage [Controlling the environment]	"You need to be able to handle any situation that's thrown at you. At the Olympics you cannot isolate yourself . . . it involves team-mates, coaches, doctors, management. You may not get on with all of them but you've got to hold it together, you have to be consistent. You may have to compete in conditions that you didn't wish for . . . you have to be able to cope with that. . . . Mentally tough performers are able to handle all the environments, all the personal and impersonal relationships, and use them to his advantage."	Negative energy control Positive energy Attitude control

Recognizing and rationalizing failure and picking out the learning points to take forward [Handling failure]	"He is able to analyze his performance and learn to adapt to whatever caused the errors so that he can reach his ultimate goal. The mentally tough performer is able to move on from that failure and it's not an issue or a mental block for him. He uses this knowledge for future performances."	Motivation Positive energy
Knowing when to celebrate success and then stop and focus on the next challenge [Handling success]	"The mentally tough performer has an acute awareness of his own ability, his levels of fitness, his strength, limitations, and what needs to be done in order to achieve the level of performance required to win. . . . He also knows when to stop celebrating and how long it will take to reach that top-level performance again."	Motivation Positive energy

Source: Adapted from G. Jones et al. (2007) and Loehr (1986).

Loehr's mental toughness attributes

According to Jim Loehr (1986), mentally tough performers are disciplined thinkers who respond to pressure in ways which enable them to remain feeling relaxed, calm, and energized because they have the ability to increase their flow of positive energy in crisis and adversity. They also have the right attitudes regarding problems, pressure, mistakes, and competition. Under competitive pressure, mentally tough performers can continue to think productively, positively, and realistically and do so with composed clarity (Loehr, 1995). Specifically, Loehr's (1986) attributes of mental toughness include: (a) self-confidence (i.e., knowing that one can perform well and be successful), (b) negative energy control (i.e., handling emotions such as fear, anger, anxiety, and frustration, and coping with externally-determined events), (c) attention control (i.e., remaining fully focused on the task at hand), (d) visualization and imagery control (i.e., thinking positively in pictures rather than words, and being able to control the flow of mental pictures and images in positive and constructive directions), (e) motivation (i.e., the ability to set meaningful goals and be willing to persevere with training schedules and to endure the pain, discomfort, and self-sacrifice associated with forward progress), (f) positive energy (i.e., the ability to become energized from such sources as fun, joy, determination, positiveness, and team spirit), and (g) attitude control (i.e., reflecting a performer's habits of thoughts, with particular emphasis on being unyielding and showing obstinate insistence on finishing rather than conceding defeat).

An enduring blueprint

Whilst recent research supports Loehr's (1986) propositions on mental toughness, this has not substantially added to the debate. There is considerable overlap between Loehr's original factors and attributes subsequently identified by other researchers that are based, to some extent, on his research (cf. G. Jones et al., 2002; Thelwell et al., 2005). For example, G. Jones et al. (p. 209) suggested that mental toughness is "having the natural or developed psychological edge that enables you to, generally, cope better than your opponents with the many demands (competition, training, lifestyle) that sport places on a performer and, specifically, be more consistent and better than your opponents in remaining determined, focused, confident, and in control under pressure." Similarly, Cashmore (2002, pp. 166–167) described mental toughness as a package of intellect qualities that includes "an unusually high level of resolution, a refusal to be intimidated, an ability to stay focused in high-pressure situations, a capacity for retaining an optimum level of arousal throughout a competition, an unflagging eagerness to compete when injured, an unyielding attitude when being beaten, a propensity to take risks when rivals show caution, and an inflexible, perhaps obstinate insistence on finishing a contest rather than conceding defeat". Interestingly, Cashmore (p. 138) shares Loehr's view that "mentally tough athletes are not emotionless: they are just skilled in subordinating emotions to the greater requirement of winning competitions". Consequently, Loehr's remains a useful and enduring blueprint for examining the construct of mental toughness. This shall be considered more closely in Chapter 3.

A mindset for all sports

As mentioned earlier in this chapter, it has been suggested that there may be inter-sport variance in mental toughness. For example, Thelwell et al. (2005) derived definitions of mental toughness that were applicable specifically to a football context (e.g., "wanting the ball at all times"). Further, G. Jones et al. (2002) proffered that a distinction should be made between emotional pain resulting from failure (arguably a sport-generic factor) and physical pain (more specific to, for example, rowing than snooker). Consequently, it has been suggested that mental toughness characteristics may be sport-specific. However, more likely is the suggestion that there exists a core set of attributes that characterize the mental toughness mindset, but that these personality characteristics can be exhibited in very different behaviours. For example, Bull et al. (2005) suggest that the maintenance of self-control at the critical moment in order to sink a short golf putt, taking calculated risks in high-speed, high-risk motor sport, the ability to handle the incredibly high volumes of training for endurance sports, and a willingness to enter into the high-intensity confrontation between batsman and bowler in cricket (and revel in it), are contrasting types of mental toughness. However, each of the scenarios above is only one behavioural response from an athlete with a mentally tough mindset. There are a multitude of other scenarios in golf (e.g., the confidence to drive over the water from a tee-shot), motor sport (e.g., the ability to hold off pursuers and maintain a lead over 60 laps), endurance sports (e.g., the ability to visualize particular components of the sport), and cricket (e.g., the ability to stick around and grind it out as a batsman when one's team-mates are losing their wickets) where another, more appropriate mentally tough response is desirable.

Not only is it the nature of the sport that elicits the appropriate behavioural manifestation of mental toughness. More accurately, it is the nature of specific scenarios at any given time in different sports that elicit the apposite response from the mentally tough performer. Some mental toughness attributes are peripheral components to the requirements of specific sports. However, the core components of mental toughness are broad enough to encompass all sports. There are equivalent expressions of mental toughness in every sport. Ultimately, at the core of the mentally tough mindset are self-belief, honesty and integrity, resolve, and a well-developed sense of ethical principles. These apply regardless of sport played.

Conclusion

Mental toughness is a notion that enjoys considerable popular appeal. As discussed in this chapter, in recent years, several researchers have devoted empirical attention to addressing the nature of mental toughness and such psychological skills used by sport performers in order to manage the stressful demands encountered in training and competition. For example, Fourie and Potgieter (2001) suggested that mentally tough performers are those athletes who have developed the necessary psychological hardiness. Mental toughness has been described as the ability to maintain an optimal mindset (J. W. Jones et al., 2001) and as a package of intellect qualities (Cashmore, 2002, 2005). For Clough et al. (2002), mentally tough performers have a high sense of self-belief, an unshakeable faith that they control their own destiny, and that such individuals remain relatively unaffected by adversity. Gould et al. (2002) described mental toughness in terms of resilience, perseverance, and the ability to deal successfully with adversity. G. Jones et al. (2002) suggested that mental toughness is having a natural or developed psychological edge that enables performers to cope with the plethora of demands made upon them. Thelwell et al. (2005) described mental toughness in terms of having a presence that affects opponents, having the ability to react to situations positively, and to be calm under, and even enjoy, pressure. While Loehr (1986) described mentally tough performers as disciplined thinkers who respond to pressure in ways which enable them to remain feeling relaxed, calm, and energized because they have the ability to increase their flow of positive energy in crisis and adversity. Such athletes also have the right attitudes regarding problems, pressure, mistakes, and competition. Mental toughness assumes effort. Mentally tough performers are effortful, tackling challenges that lie just beyond their competence.

This chapter has presented the characteristics historically associated with mental toughness within the extant literature. Acknowledging the widespread use of the term mental toughness by sport psychologists, researchers in sport psychology, coaches, and performers, the present chapter has examined the concept in terms of how it is defined and its constitutive attributes. The present chapter has shown that, within the literature, there is common agreement that accomplished sport performers are mentally tough. Despite the breadth of constitutive attributes, a consensus is emerging as to what is characteristic of mental toughness. For sure, there is a strong argument that this collection of characteristics represents a particular mindset. The debate over a definition of mental toughness can now be advanced to an examination of its conceptual clarification. Specifically, Chapter 3 will consider the multi-faceted role of mental toughness and question an emerging conceptualization that its sole function is that as a moderator of the stress response.

3 Conceptualizing mental toughness

> Men are not disturbed by things, but by the view they take of them.
>
> Epictetus

Introduction

The potentially stressful nature of being involved in competitive sport is well documented. Athletes participating in training and competition frequently encounter stressors, whether in individual (e.g., Cohn, 1990; Giacobbi, Foore, & Weinberg, 2004; Giacobbi, Lynn, Wetherington, Jenkins, Bodendorf, & Langley, 2004; McKay, Niven, Lavallee, & White, 2008; Nicholls, Holt, & Polman, 2005) or team (e.g., Anshel, 2001; Holt & Hogg, 2002; Nicholls, Holt, Polman, & Bloomfield, 2006; Noblet & Gifford, 2002; Noblet, Rodwell, & McWilliams, 2003) sport environments. Sport performers, particularly those operating at the highest professional levels, must cope with the stressors they experience in order to sustain high levels of performance and maintain their status. Participating in competitive sport requires athletes not only to develop and maintain a high level of sport ability, but also to assemble a collection of skills to cope with stressful encounters in a challenging environment. To this end, the lessons of success in sport are often linked with the ability to display mental toughness in stressful situations.

Mental toughness as a moderator of stress

As discussed in Chapter 2, for many researchers of mental toughness, a strong mindset exists in relation to overcoming adversity (e.g., Dorfman, 2003; Fourie & Potgieter, 2001; G. Jones et al., 2002; Middleton et al., 2004a; Thelwell et al., 2005). In a recent study of the stressors facing cricketers (Thelwell, Weston, & Greenlees, 2007), reported coping strategies included: "see the pressure as a challenge", "tell myself to fight", "tell myself to focus", "tell myself to be patient", "tell myself to control the controllables", "be ice cold to the opposition", "stay level headed", "maintain composure", "get myself calm before a game", and "look for a confrontation". Each of these is constitutive of mental toughness. Others have pursued this direction. For example, Fletcher (2005) conceptualized mental toughness as "an individual's propensity to manage the demands of environmental stressors, ranging from an absolute resilience to extreme vulnerability" (p. 1246). He argued that it represents a composite variable that is a conglomerate of the more manifest moderators of the stress process. Further, Fletcher suggested that a complete understanding of mental toughness and human performance would only be obtained if it were studied within the context of a transactional conceptualization of stress.

Fletcher's (2005) facet model outlines the moderating role of mental toughness in the stress process and its theoretical relationship with performance (Figure 3.1). According to the model, the relevance of the attributes that constitute mental toughness will depend on the combination of different personal, organizational, and competitive stressors encountered by performers in a particular situation. These attributes moderate the relationship between stressors and responses by influencing athletes' appraisal and coping. Mental toughness, therefore, plays a pivotal role in determining how athletes cognitively, emotionally, and behaviourally respond to stressors, which will in turn affect their performance.

Developing the idea of mental toughness as a moderator of the stress response, Fletcher and Fletcher (2005) offered a supraordinate perspective of the stress–emotion–performance relationship. The authors proposed that stressors arise from the

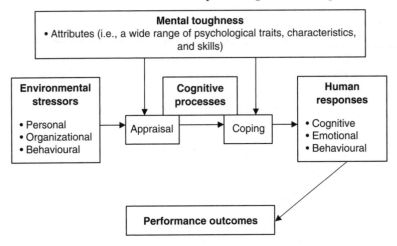

Figure 3.1 A facet model of mental toughness and human performance.
Source: Adapted from Fletcher (2005), reprinted by permission of Taylor & Francis Ltd, www.informaworld.com.

environment in which athletes operate, are mediated by the processes of perception, appraisal, and coping, and, consequently, result in positive or negative responses, feeling states, and outcomes. They added that this is an ongoing process, moderated by various personal and situational factors, including athletes' levels of mental toughness. With regard to causal sequence, it could be argued that the ability to withstand stress is an indication of a mentally tough performer, and that, consequently, being mentally tough is predictive of the ability to handle stress.

The aforementioned conceptualization of mental toughness has much in common with the Cognitive-Affective Processing System (CAPS) model of personality advanced by Walter Mischel and Yuichi Shoda (Mischel & Shoda, 1995). This model accounts for personality coherence in terms of a stable system, whose functioning underlies both consistency and situationally-based variability in behaviour. It is a dynamic network of cognitive, affective, motivational, and behaviour-generation units that interacts with situational factors to produce both coherence and cross-situational variability in behaviour. Within the CAPS framework, mentally tough performers are likely to exhibit the following characteristics:

they encode demanding situations as challenges and opportunities, rather than threats; they confidently view themselves as having the personal resources needed to cope successfully with pressure situations; and they feel in control of self and capable of producing a positive outcome.

According to the CAPS model, mentally tough athletes also have a distinctive motivational structure. Their goals include seeking out challenging situations with uncertain outcomes. They value personal improvement and skill mastery, are high in positive achievement motivation, and relatively low in fear of failure. Mentally tough athletes are also self-motivated and self-directed in their efforts to improve; and they do not require external pressure to work hard. Their commitment to their sport often sets them apart.

The affective responses of mentally tough athletes facilitate rather than impair performance by enhancing their ability to remain focused on the task at hand under even the most demanding and potentially distracting conditions. Their self-reinforcement standards involve giving maximum effort at all times, especially in the face of adversity. Self-standards are self-referenced, realistic, and oriented toward skill improvement. They have the self-regulation skills needed to persist in the face of adversity, and their ability to delay gratification contributes to the commitment they exhibit to skill development. Mentally tough athletes know how to develop action plans, how to learn, and how to improve. All of these characteristics facilitate their development and performance under pressure. Interestingly, within the CAPS framework, reference is made to personality "hardiness": mentally tough performers are able to function in the face of difficulties that would interfere with the performance of less hardy individuals (Mischel & Shoda, 1995).

Developing this connection, particularly noteworthy is the conclusion of Fourie and Potgieter (2001, p. 71) that "athletes should develop the necessary psychological hardiness". Indeed, psychological hardiness was one of the 12 umbrella mental toughness categories identified in that study and was defined as the "ability of the athlete to reveal a strong personality, emotional and psychological well-being, to take charge, and show autonomy" (p. 68). Similarly, Clough et al. (2002, p. 38), writing of mentally tough performers, stated that: "with a high sense of self-belief and an unshakeable faith that they control their own destiny, these individuals can remain relatively unaffected by competition or adversity". This definition suggests operationalizing mental toughness in terms of psychological resilience or stress-resistance; in effect, individuals' positive responses to situations of stress and adversity (Braddock, Royster, Winfield, & Hawkins, 1991; Rutter, 1987; Tugade & Fredrickson, 2004). Though the aforementioned descriptions of hardiness are in stark contrast to that originally put forward by Suzanne Kobasa (1979), such resilient responses have often been described in terms of demonstrations of the hardy personality. Moreover, some researchers have attempted to define mental toughness within the theoretical context of Kobasa's hardiness model.

The relationship between mental toughness and hardiness

The term "hardiness" has often been used to describe stress-resistant individuals. With its stress-buffering (e.g., Kobasa, 1979; Maddi, Kahn, & Maddi, 1998; Wiebe, 1991) and performance-enhancing (e.g., Atella, 1999; Westman, 1990) functions, the moderating effects of this construct have become associated with those purported of mental toughness (cf. Clough et al., 2002; Golby & Sheard, 2004, 2006; Golby et al., 2003; Sheard & Golby, 2006a, 2006b). Further, the environments in which the moderating effects of hardiness have been demonstrated make sport a similarly promising potential source of empirical enquiry for the conceptualization of mental toughness. Thus, it seems plausible that mental toughness and hardiness share the same conceptual space.

Conceptualizing hardiness

The hardiness construct, with its roots in existential theory (e.g., Frankl, 1959; Gendlin, 1966; Kierkegaard, 1843/1959), emerged from individual differences research on stress reactions, and has been conceptualized as a combination of the three attitudes (3Cs) of *commitment*, *control*, and *challenge* (Kobasa, 1979; Maddi, 2006). Hardiness provides the existential courage that aids the individual in pursuing the future despite its uncertainty (Maddi, 2004; Tillich,

1952). *Commitment* (vs. alienation) epitomizes those individuals who are committed to and feel deeply involved in the activities of their lives. People high in *commitment* get involved rather than withdraw, seeing this as the best way to turn their environments and whatever they are experiencing into something that seems interesting, worthwhile, and important, regardless of how stressful things become (Maddi, 2006; Maddi, Khoshaba, Persico, Lu, Harvey, & Bleecker, 2002). *Control* (vs. powerlessness) reflects people's desire to continue to have an influence on the outcomes going on around them, no matter how difficult and stressful this becomes (Maddi, 2006). Hardy individuals control the events of their experience in terms of what they choose to do and how they choose to respond to various events (Maddi, 1990). *Challenge* (vs. security) typifies an expectation that life is unpredictable and that changes will stimulate personal development. Potentially stressful situations are appraised as exciting and stimulating rather than threatening, enabling people to feel positively about life's fluctuations. People high in *challenge* believe that what improves their lives is growth through learning rather than easy comfort and security (Maddi, 2006).

According to Salvatore Maddi and Deborah Khoshaba, hardy individuals construct meaning in their lives by recognizing that (a) everything they do constitutes a decision, (b) decisions invariably involve pushing toward the future or shrinking into the past, and (c) choosing the future expands meaning, whereas choosing the past contracts it (Maddi & Khoshaba, 2001). Though positive in terms of meaning and possibilities, choosing the future raises anxiety over the unpredictable nature of things not yet experienced. Almost every decision we make entails predicting the future. To accept this so-called ontological anxiety and push ahead with choosing the future anyway requires the courage that is the manifestation of existentialist theory. Adoption of such a philosophy helps us to accept that "life is full of risks. It is pretty much all there is to life: it is a ribbon of uncertainty that one day suddenly runs out" (Joseph, 2008). Substituting courage with hardiness lends precision to the existential formulation by emphasizing the three inter-related beliefs about one's interaction with the world: *commitment*, *control*, and *challenge*.

As conceptualized, the 3Cs of hardiness are a cognitive/ emotional/behavioural amalgam constituting a learned, growth-oriented, personality style. Hardiness theory submits that people who feel committed, in control, and positively challenged by life circumstances have the tendency to perceive events or circumstances as less stressful, seeing them as manageable rather than overwhelming (Khoshaba & Maddi, 1999). Performance of these individuals is enhanced by their active or decisive coping efforts in stressful situations (Soderstrom, Dolbier, Leiferman, & Steinhardt, 2000). As such, hardiness is a pathway to resilience under stress (Bonanno, 2004). The positive influence of hardiness on performance has been reported in such diverse samples as athletes (Golby & Sheard, 2004; Golby et al., 2003; Sheard, 2008a; Sheard & Golby, 2006a; Sheard & Golby, 2007a, Sheard & Golby, in press), human resource consultants (Maddi, Harvey, Khoshaba, Lu, Persico, & Brow, 2006), military personnel (Bartone, 1999), and university undergraduates (Sheard, 2009; Sheard & Golby, 2007b).

Some people have a "hardy" personality in the sense that they possess, for example, coping skills that enable them to thrive in adverse circumstances. Kobasa's (1979) hardy personality style serves as a useful theoretical model for the construct validity of mental toughness. Characteristics of the hardy personality are consistent with those of mentally tough performers, identified earlier in Chapter 2. For example, consistent with findings for hardiness (e.g., Khoshaba & Maddi, 1999), recent research has shown a positive association between higher levels of mental toughness and problem or approach coping strategies (Nicholls, Polman, Levy, & Backhouse, 2008). Similarly, the stress-buffering and performance-enhancement benefits derived from possession of a hardy personality style are congruous with those of mentally tough individuals (cf. Clough et al., 2002; Fourie & Potgieter, 2001; G. Jones et al., 2002; R. E. Smith & Smoll, 1989; R. M. Williams, 1988). Indeed, past research has synonymized mental toughness with cognitive hardiness (e.g., Hollander & Acevedo, 2000; R. E. Smith, 2006). Thus, for some researchers, the relationship with Kobasa's model of hardiness has served as an appropriate theoretical frame of reference for the conceptualization of mental toughness.

Conceptualizing mental toughness using the hardiness model

Kobasa's (1979) model (i.e., a commitment to be fully involved in one's environment; a sense of control over it; and a view of the future which approaches it with a sense of challenge, rather than with feelings of apprehension) has been employed to show links between hardiness and mental toughness. For example, Clough et al. (2002) provided support for the 3Cs of hardiness, but also revealed the importance of a fourth attitude (namely, confidence) to reflect the transposition of the related construct of hardiness into the more sport-specific concept of mental toughness. According to Clough et al., hardiness fails "to capture the unique nature of the physical and mental demands of competitive sport" (p. 37). However, their transposition of hardiness to mental toughness was not fully justified. In particular, the authors did not provide a rationale as to why mental toughness is a sport-specific form of hardiness. Further, the 3Cs hardiness model assumes confidence to be implicit across the three hardiness attitudes (Maddi & Khoshaba, 2001).

More than a pathway to resilience under stress

Undoubtedly, the mentally tough mindset includes an ability to bounce back from stressful experiences quickly and effectively. However, if the sole function of mental toughness is as a moderator of the stress response, then the construct is little different to psychological resilience, in that it is the demonstration of effective coping and adaptation in the face of loss, hardship, or adversity (Rutter, 1999; Tugade & Frederickson, 2004). Refusing to give in is a fine characteristic; but I believe the mental toughness mindset offers more.

It is assumed that many elite performers possess mentally tough qualities such as resilience and an ability to experience stress and cope with it to maintain and to enhance their performance. However, it could also be claimed that athletes are likely to require other mental toughness attributes that need not necessarily manifest exclusively in adversity. Arguably, the most important finding in a study of mental toughness in Australian Rules football was that mental toughness was considered important not only for those situations with negative effects (e.g., injury, de-selection), but also for some situations with positive effects (e.g., good form, previous season champions) (Gucciardi et al., 2008).

Previous conceptualizations of mental toughness have focused too heavily on the notion of adversity and how the key components enable athletes to deal with and overcome such setbacks. Mental toughness involves having to deal with, and overcome, situations with negative effects, but it also enables individuals to flourish in situations where there are positive effects and perceived positive pressure. Defined in this sense, mental toughness can be conceptualized not only as a buffer against adversity, but as a collection of inter-related protective and enabling attributes that promote and maintain adaptation to other positive, though challenging, situations.

Support for this is provided in an investigation of mental toughness and sport performers' goal orientation. A study by Kuan and Roy (2007) that recruited 40 Malaysian athletes revealed that individuals with a high task/moderate ego goal profile had greater mental toughness in controlling negative energy than athletes with a moderate task/low ego goal profile. High task/moderate ego athletes were also significantly higher in positive energy when compared to moderate task/moderate ego performers. Results also suggest the possibility that athletes with a high task/moderate ego goal profile probably benefit during adversities in competition, due to good self-control, leading to greater mental toughness.

A mindset for all situations

At some time throughout their career, athletes are likely to experience stress and cope with it to maintain and enhance their performance. This notwithstanding, there is more to mental toughness than its function as a defence mechanism against adversity. Gucciardi et al. (2008) suggest that, within Australian Rules football at least, mental toughness is a collection of values, attitudes, behaviours, and emotions that facilitate performers' perseverance in adverse situations. But they add that it is also the ability to maintain concentration and motivation to achieve goals. The athletes interviewed in the Gucciardi et al. study stated that thorough preparation made a substantial contribution to their self-belief. In addition, an exceptional work ethic characterized by determination, perseverance, and time-management was considered vital in not only overcoming adversities, but also surmounting them quicker and better than expected (e.g., injury rehabilitation).

Interestingly, professionals operating in rugby league football have conceptualized mental toughness similarly. In addition to performers having the ability to handle pressure and thrive in adverse circumstances, Salford City Reds head coach Shaun McRae suggested a good work ethic and collective responsibility are also constitutive of mental toughness (personal communication, November 28, 2007). McRae added: "Mental toughness is the ability of athletes to take themselves out of their comfort zone. Such athletes perform to their ability against adversity, stress, or pressures, when other athletes tend to make mistakes and lose focus. Also, mentally tough athletes generally achieve their goals, hold their nerve, and always lead by action rather than words." Stressing that mental toughness included possession of an unyielding mindset, he also articulated that mentally tough performers understand the consequences of quitting. Senior professional and club captain Malcolm Alker corroborated his coach's conceptualization: "Mental toughness is the ability of athletes to take their body and mind to a place where it hurts and where they don't really want to be, but know it's the only way to achieve their goals. Athletes are willing to make sacrifices to overcome adversity and negativity to realize their talent" (personal communication, December 19, 2007). Similarly, iconic New Zealand international Robbie Paul spoke of mental toughness in terms of "senior players creating a mentally tough environment . . . learning from life's experiences . . . and a high work ethic" (personal communication, November 28, 2007).

Mental toughness as psychological preparation

Clearly, as conceptualized above, such attributes of mental toughness need not be shown only in adverse circumstances. It is also apparent that mental toughness is a multi-factorial construct, with its constitutive factors manifested behaviourally either singularly or in combination in response to the appropriate situation or context. Such a conceptualization is remarkably similar to the work of the pioneering Soviet sport psychologist Avksenty Cezarevich Puni. He wrote of the psychological preparation of athletes for competition, yet it could so easily be read as a blueprint for mental toughness. Puni (1963) stated that sport performers need a sensible confidence in their abilities, the readiness to overcome all obstacles, including unexpected ones of various degrees of difficulty, the active aspiration to strive passionately to achieve not only the set goal but also the highest result possible, the appropriate level of emotional arousal, and the ability to control one's own thoughts, feelings, and behaviours. Collectively, these components were termed *boevaya gotovnost*, or "readiness to fight".

Mental toughness as a life skill

Respondents in a recent study felt that the attributes associated with mentally tough performers could facilitate life outside of sport (Connaughton, Wadey, Hanton, & Jones, 2008). As conceptualized, mental toughness could be explored as a life skill. The study's authors suggested that this is particularly relevant if athletes' concerns relate as much to broader life issues as to specific sport performance matters. This supports the Middleton et al. (2004a) model that suggests mental toughness has broad relevance. Indeed, it is difficult to conceive why mental toughness should be a mindset relevant only in sport situations, rather than a personality style that more broadly allows individuals to deal effectively with life's myriad circumstances.

A positive psychological perspective

The aforementioned constitutive characteristics suggest that mental toughness be considered within the framework of "positive psychology" (Seligman & Csikszentmihalyi, 2000). Psychology has traditionally been characterized by a pathogenic paradigm in what Barnard (1994, p. 136) called "an obsessive proclivity for 'deficit detecting' to the exclusion of acknowledging strengths and resources". However, emerging from humanistic theory, positive psychology offers an alternative context that concentrates on positive experiences and positive character or virtues.

Positive psychology

The positive psychology movement suggests that psychology since World War II has been sidetracked by an over-emphasis on mental illness from its other two important missions – making the lives of all people more fulfilling, and identifying and nurturing high talent. Optimal functioning, such as superior sport performance, cannot be understood within a purely problem-oriented framework. In contrast to the pathological interest in "what can go wrong", there have also been ongoing attempts to discover "what can go right" (Basic Behavioral Science Task Force, 1996, p. 23). Compared to a psychology as "victimology", the new positive paradigm is turning it into a "science of strength" (Seligman & Csikszentmihalyi, 2000, pp. 6, 8), "a fascination with strengths" (Saleeby, 1997, p. 4), and a "psychology of survivorship, resiliency, encouragement, and strength" (Abi-Hashem, 2001, p. 86).

Martin Seligman and Mihaly Csikszentmihalyi have called for the study of psychology to move beyond psychological disorders and problems and for greater efforts to be spent on positive psychology; that is, how psychology can be used to facilitate human functioning (Seligman & Csikszentmihalyi, 2000). Facilitating human performance is the primary goal of the sport psychologist, with much research in the field of sport psychology focusing considerable attention on what it takes to be a great athlete. Thus, positive psychology is an appropriate theoretical framework within which researchers can explore further the relationship between mental toughness and superior sport performance (Gould, 2002).

Indeed, several researchers have conceptualized mental toughness such that it reflects the positive psychology paradigm. G. Jones et al. (2007) commented on "a diverse range of positive psychological characteristics being associated with mental toughness" (p. 244). One of Middleton et al.'s (2004a) 12 key mental toughness characteristics included "believing in your own potential and capacity for growth and development". Bull et al. (2005) also recognized mental toughness as a positive psychological construct. Moreover, their positive psychological framework of mental toughness is now an integral part of the English Cricket Board's Level 3 and 4 coaching qualifications. Further, several studies have revealed numerous positive psychological constructs as key correlates of mental toughness; for example, dispositional optimism, self-efficacy, self-esteem, and positive/negative affectivity (cf. Clough et al., 2002; Golby & Sheard, 2006; Nicholls et al., 2008; Sheard & Golby, 2006a, 2006b).

The study of optimal functioning, human strengths, and positive psychological outcomes is growing rapidly (Kahneman, Diener, & Schwartz, 1999; Seligman & Csikszentmihalyi, 2000). Termed the scientific study of human strengths and happiness (Seligman & Csikszentmihalyi), positive psychology focuses on individuals' resilience, resourcefulness, and capacity for renewal. The subsequent application of this focus is to facilitate optimal functioning (Linley & Joseph, 2004). The belief that, for example, athletes are shaped not by the experience itself, but by their perception of that experience makes positive psychology a particularly appealing theoretical context in which to frame mental toughness. Indeed, the constituent components of mental toughness sit comfortably alongside the classified positive psychological character strengths; namely, wisdom and knowledge, courage, humanity, justice, temperance, and transcendence (see Peterson & Seligman, 2004).

Given that sport performers will face experiences throughout their careers, positive psychology theory implies that personality has the potential to develop and the capacity to improve. For example, some people are better at handling failure than others. Some also are able to recover and find ways of improving, while others feel inhibited and frustrated. A central tenet of the positive psychology paradigm is that stressors, adversity, and other inordinate demands are inherent to the human condition. However, the paradigm assumes that there are also sources of strength, through which this condition can be endured and even transcended. Physical, emotional, and social stressors can stimulate growth and strengthening in many individuals. Such people are often able to tap into previously unknown capacities, perspectives, and virtues. Mental toughness distinguishes people in these behaviours. In this context, addressing the question of why some sportspeople are mentally tougher than others is important for both theoretical and practical reasons, and should be a central goal of a comprehensive positive psychology.

The call for psychology to devote more attention to facilitating optimal human functioning (Seligman & Csikszentmihalyi, 2000), and for this to be achieved through the application of positive psychology (Linley & Joseph, 2004), is being increasingly heeded in the sporting domain. The positive psychology movement's assertion that "psychology is not just the study of pathology, weakness, and damage; it is also the study of strength and virtue. Treatment is not just fixing what is broken; it is nurturing what is best" (Seligman & Csikszentmihalyi, p. 7), is an obviously desirable theoretical frame of reference within which to carry out further research with regard to the construct validation of mental toughness.

Conclusion

This chapter has conceptualized the term "mental toughness" and, via its proposed relationship with hardiness, that the behavioural manifestation of the mentally tough mindset incorporates mechanisms that afford resilient individuals the opportunity to overcome stress or adversity. It is assumed that the positive orientation toward life afforded by hardiness helps individuals to stay healthy and to maintain successful performance under stressful circumstances. Moreover, mental toughness involves multiple cognitive and motivational processes that moderate the impact of the objective environment and ameliorate performance (Lyubomirsky, 2001).

The mental toughness mindset advocated in this chapter reflects the model suggested by Loehr (1986) that mental toughness is predicated on the feeling that one is in control (as a result of good preparation and a high level of commitment) and is able to thrive on the pressure of competition. Similarly, performers interviewed by Gould et al. (2002) described mental toughness as attending to what one can control, and the demonstration of perseverance, resilience, and persistence in the face of difficulties. Further support may be derived from definitional comments reported by G. Jones et al. (2002, p. 212); for example, "not getting unsettled by things you didn't expect or can't control; the mentally tough performer is able to compose himself and come back and still win; mental toughness is using the competition pressure to get the best out of yourself".

The key point here is that mental toughness characteristics are not shown exclusively in adverse circumstances. There is more to mental toughness than mere reaction. Mental toughness is as much concerned with the mindset that performers bring to training and competition as it is with reacting to, and coping with, stressful situations. In addition to having the ability to cope (and thrive) in stressful and adverse circumstances, it is clear from the evidence proffered in this chapter that mentally tough athletes possess self-belief, determination, motivation, competitiveness, and a high work ethic; each of which can be demonstrated long before athletes need to deal with adverse situations. Further, mental toughness is not sport-specific. Rather, it is a core set of attributes constitutive of a mentally tough mindset. Attributes specific to any particular sport are on the periphery.

In a nutshell, mental toughness is a mindset and stable disposition that captures the cognitive, emotional, and behavioural characteristics of top sport performers. I would argue that mental toughness reflects a lived and experienced philosophy, applied to each situation encountered. Therefore, it is a global disposition. And I say this because mental toughness is both an active and a moderating variable. Manifestations of mental toughness in as many contexts as possible is desirable; not only in sport, but in home life, work life, all aspects.

Finally, given the definitional consensus on athletes' resilience, resourcefulness, and capacity for renewal, this chapter proposed that mental toughness be considered within the positive psychology paradigm (Seligman & Csikszentmihalyi, 2000). Moving away from a pathogenic or deficit model, this movement observes positive outcomes in the face of adversity, giving consideration to the development processes that lead to both physical and mental health and well-being instead (Schoon & Bartley, 2008). Clearly, this positive psychology paradigm is an appropriate and desirable theoretical frame of reference within which to consider mental toughness.

Acknowledging the widespread use of the term mental toughness by sport psychologists, coaches, performers, and the media, the present chapter has examined the construct in terms of its conceptualization. Despite the volume of qualitative research (see Chapter 2), insufficient effort has been devoted to the development of a reliable and valid measure of mental toughness in sport. Indeed, an obstacle in the path of further empirical work on mental toughness has been the apparent lack of suitable inventories. As the following chapter shows, there have been developmental difficulties with inventories purporting to measure mental toughness. However, this is no longer the case. Revealed in Chapter 4, there are, finally, psychometrically acceptable instruments that measure mental toughness.

4 Measuring mental toughness

This is courage in a man to bear unflinchingly what heaven sends.

Euripides

Introduction

The nature of psychological profiling, and, for example, its potential for predicting potentially successful athletes, has prompted researchers to engage in the design of psychometric instruments capable of measuring the range of skills thought to underlie sport performance (M. Wilkinson & Ashford, 1997). Indeed, the use of psychometric testing to provide psychological profiles is moving progressively from business into sport (Hotten, 2003). However, there is only limited evidence concerning mental toughness predicting success in a variety of competitive sporting environments. Given that the literature dedicated to mental toughness has been characterized by a general lack of conceptual clarity and consensus over its definition, as covered in the previous chapters, there has been difficulty in developing a suitable measure of the construct. Addressing, in particular, Aidan Moran's (2004) critical observation that mental toughness lacks an independent index, this chapter discusses attempts to develop psychometrically acceptable quantitative measures of mental toughness.

Mental toughness as a subscale of other measures

Research has suggested that athletes tend to be more "tough-minded" than the average population (Eysenck, Nias, & Cox, 1982; Kirkcaldy, 1985). However, tough-minded in these studies was determined by higher scores on some scales (e.g., dominance, risk taking, psychoticism, sensation seeking), and by greater emotional stability as measured by lower scores on anxiety and neuroticism scales, not by a measure of mental toughness itself. Similarly, the phrase "tough-mindedness" has been used to describe the determination and resolve of high-performance climbers (Egan & Stelmack, 2003). Attempts have also been made to measure mental toughness as a bipolar personality style (Shafer, 1999). Researchers using the Comrey Personality Scales (CPS; Comrey, 1994) have described mental toughness as a primary trait loading onto three higher-order factors (namely, extraversion, conscientiousness, empathy) within a general personality factor (Rushton & Irwing, 2009). However, the five variables pertaining to the mental toughness versus sensitivity subscale on the CPS bear no resemblance to the instrument's potential utility in a sport domain (e.g., no fear of bugs, no crying, no romantic love, tolerance of blood, and tolerance of vulgarity). Thus, as this scale was not designed specifically for sport, the appropriateness of such variables as measurements of mental toughness in a sport environment is questionable (Gill, Dzewaltowksi, & Deeter, 1988). Moreover, given the complexity of the mental toughness construct (as annotated in Chapters 2 and 3), viewing sensitivity as the "opposite" of mental toughness is, arguably, simplistic.

Other studies have developed sport-specific questionnaires with the purpose of assessing, among other psychological skills, mental toughness. For example, Patrick Thomas and co-workers developed the Ten-Pin Bowling Performance Survey (Thomas, Schlinker, & Over, 1996). The substantive section of the questionnaire was designed to obtain information on psychological and psychomotor skills in ten-pin bowling and involvement in the sport. Each item was worded with direct reference to ten-pin bowling. Thus, respondents ($N = 172$ bowlers; 87 males, 85 females) did not rate mental toughness in general, but mental toughness when bowling.

Table 4.1 Ten-Pin Bowling Performance Survey mental toughness items

Mental toughness subscale item	Factor loading
Play best under pressure of competition	.67
Concentration is easily broken	−.64
Mentally tough competitor at bowling	.61
Play better at practice than competition	−.57
Difficulty "handling the pace" frames 8, 9, 10	−.55
Come from behind to win a match	.52
Difficult to refocus attention after distraction	−.51
Concentrate for extended periods	.49
Not easily distracted during delivery	.42
Unsettled by what other players say and do	−.40
Self-talk during competition is negative	−.37

Source: Adapted from Thomas et al. (1996) reprinted by permission of Taylor & Francis Ltd, www.informaworld.com.

The items (e.g., "I am a mentally tough competitor at bowling") were each rated on a 5-point scale ranging from "strongly disagree" to "strongly agree".

Factor analysis of responses to 37 items in the Ten-Pin Bowling Performance Survey yielded five component measures of psychological skills, accounting for 41 per cent of the variance. The scale's third factor was labelled "mental toughness", and evaluated concentration and coping with pressure during competitive bowling. Five items were positively worded and six items were negatively worded. The 11 items relating to the mental toughness subscale, along with their factor loadings, are shown in Table 4.1.

The mental toughness subscale had a .80 coefficient alpha for internal reliability, and a .87 test–retest correlation coefficient. Predictive validity was demonstrated as skilled bowlers rated themselves significantly higher ($p < .001$) on mental toughness than their less-skilled counterparts. The efficacy of mental toughness in helping to maintain optimum performance under adverse circumstances is also evident in statements by elite bowlers such as United States PBA champions Dick Weber ("every bowler who wins a lot thrives on pressure") and Carmen Salvino ("I love it when I need a double to win"). Successful players like these report that they perform well under pressure, have no difficulty "handling the pace", can concentrate for extended periods, and often come from behind to win (Herbst, 1986). Thus, prowess at ten-pin bowling is associated with high levels of mental toughness.

Developed by Gershon Tenenbaum and colleagues, the Running Discomfort Scale (Tenenbaum et al., 1999) sought to elicit feelings and thoughts of people engaged in running activities. The final version of the questionnaire consisted of 32 items divided into eight correlated subscales. Mental toughness was the seventh subscale, consisting of items 30 and 31, and had a coefficient alpha of .63. These items had factor loadings of .79 and .75, respectively, accounting for 3.4 per cent variance out of a total 63.6 per cent variance. The authors defined mentally tough runners as those who were "psychologically strong" and were capable of "intense concentration".

The motivational-affective second-order dimension yielded by Tenenbaum et al. (1999) was associated with motivation during the discomfort state; therefore, the authors suggested that: "'mental toughness' is conceptually associated with this global dimension" (p. 194). Particularly noteworthy from the findings of this study was the assertion that mental toughness had a strategic role: "Runners in distance races are more concerned with task completion and mental toughness strategies than with physical discomfort symptoms coming from their legs, respiratory system, proprioceptive systems, and head and stomach" (p. 194). The authors concluded that under such conditions of perceived discomfort, the mechanisms for the regulation of pain are more likely to stem from psychological (e.g., mental toughness) than physical bases.

Development of questionnaires to assess mental toughness

The Sports Performance Inventory

The Sports Performance Inventory (SPI; J. W. Jones et al., 2001) is a sport-specific attitudinal measure. Exploratory factor analysis of data from 274 US university athletes on an 83-item survey yielded six interpretable factors; namely, competitiveness, team orientation, emotional control, positive attitude, safety consciousness, and mental toughness. All subscale reliability estimates were .79 or higher. However, no further published psychometric data are available for the SPI, and, crucially, there remains the need for the inventory to be subjected to confirmatory factor analyses. Several of the SPI's 17 mental toughness items share features with Loehr's (1986) blueprint. For example, the item "I have trouble handling the pressure of important competitions" reflects Loehr's *negative energy control* subscale. However, the SPI mental toughness subscale fails to capture the breadth of the constitutive components of mental toughness.

The Mental Toughness 48

The Mental Toughness 48 (MT48; Clough et al., 2002) was developed by Peter Clough and colleagues to operationalize their own 4Cs model of mental toughness. The scale contains 48 items that are scored on a 5-point Likert scale ranging from "strongly agree" to "strongly disagree", with an average completion time between 10 and 15 minutes. The MT48 yields scores for overall mental toughness and on each of the inventory's four subscales; namely, commitment, control, challenge, and confidence. The first three components of the MT48 reflect the authors' attempt to define mental toughness within the theoretical framework of Kobasa's (1979) hardiness.

The instrument has been used in studies of mental toughness (e.g., Simpson, Gray, & Florida-James, 2006). However, as only minimal psychometric information is available, its usefulness is questionable. The instrument has an overall test–retest coefficient of .90, with the internal consistency of the subscales found to be .71, .73, .71, and .80 for commitment, control, challenge, and confidence, respectively. Alongside the MT48, Clough et al. (2002) developed the MT18 (a shorter 18-item version), "to make it more accessible and usable for the end-user (sports people)" (p. 39). The two instruments have shown a strong correlation ($r = .87$; Clough et al.). However, the MT18 provides only an overall score for mental toughness and not a profile of subscales, as with the MT48.

The MT48 has recently been refined and relabelled as the MTQ48. The modifications apply to the control and confidence subscales; that is, emotional control and life control, and interpersonal confidence and confidence in abilities. Using the updated instrument on a non-sport sample of 544 participants, an overall coefficient alpha of .89 for the scale was reported (Marchant, Clough, Polman, Levy, & Strycharczyk, 2007). A subsequent study, using 677 athletes, reported an overall coefficient alpha of .87 for the scale, with individual subscales ranging from .58 to .71, suggesting only satisfactory reliability (Nicholls et al., 2008).

Whether as the original (MT48) or the modified (MTQ48) version, there is little published evidence of the scale's psychometric properties. Although the construct (MT48, Clough et al., 2002; MTQ48, Nicholls et al., 2008) and criterion (MT48, Clough et al.; Crust & Clough, 2005; MTQ48, Marchant et al., 2007) validity of both versions appear to have been established, to date, there has been no further published independent research examining the instrument's psychometric properties. Its factor structure, in particular, has not been rigorously scrutinized using exploratory and confirmatory techniques. Further, the scale's authors offered little rationale for the association with hardiness, which, ultimately, is the basis for the instrument's subscales.

The Mental Toughness Inventory

The Mental Toughness Inventory (MTI; Middleton, Marsh, Martin, Richards, & Perry, 2004b), developed by Cory Middleton and co-workers, is a 65-item instrument that measures 12 components of mental toughness alongside global mental toughness. The authors piloted the questionnaire that operationalized their definition of mental toughness (Middleton et al., 2004a). Middleton et al. (2004b) recruited 479 elite student athletes to complete the pilot MTI (117 items). A series of confirmatory factor analyses produced the 13-factor 65-item scale. A 5-item-per-factor solution yielded the best fit (root mean square of approximation (RMSEA) = .065, Tucker–Lewis index (TLI) = .973, relative noncentrality index (RNI) = .975). The reliability coefficients for each of the factors ranged from .87 to .95. Each of the 12 factors correlated strongly with global mental toughness, with correlations ranging from $r = .45$ to $r = .87$. The MTI appears to have been developed from a sound theoretical base and has been evaluated via a construct validation framework. Recent research has used the scale to examine the relationship between mental toughness attributes and changes in stress-recovery imbalance associated with a competition break (Tibbert, Morris, & Andersen, 2009). However, few other details of the scale are available. Moreover, that the scale has been validated using only elite sport high school athletes with a mean age of just 14 years (range 12 to 19 years) appears to be a limitation. Future testing of the MTI is needed in order to determine its predictive (e.g., elite vs. non-elite athletes) validity.

The Mental Toughness Scale

Designed by Andrew Lane and colleagues, the Mental Toughness Scale (MTS; Lane et al., 2007) was developed from qualitative data from elite athletes and was an attempt to capture the nature of mental toughness as described by G. Jones et al. (2002). The result was a 27-item measure in which items were rated on a 7-point Likert scale anchored by "not at all" and "very much so". Forward multiple regression indicated that optimism, social skills, and appraisal of one's own emotions accounted for 60 per cent of the variance in mental toughness, as measured by the MTS. However, only 75 participants completed the inventory. Also, other than correlations with a measure of emotional intelligence, the authors fail to report any further details of the scale's psychometric properties.

The Australian football Mental Toughness Inventory

Created by Daniel Gucciardi and co-workers, the Australian football Mental Toughness Inventory (AfMTI; Gucciardi, Gordon, & Dimmock, 2009) is a 24-item scale that measures four components of mental toughness in Australian Rules football; namely, thrive through challenge, sport awareness, tough attitude, and desire success. Preliminary data on the factor structure, internal reliability, and construct validity of the scale are encouraging. The authors also found no evidence that the football players sampled were giving socially desirable responses (Gucciardi et al.). However, further and more stringent psychometric examinations must be conducted before the AfMTI can be considered a useful tool for measuring mental toughness. It must be stressed also that the scale has been designed for use solely in the domain of Australian Rules football.

The Mental, Emotional, and Bodily Toughness Inventory

The Mental, Emotional, and Bodily Toughness Inventory (MeBTough), developed by Mack and Ragan (2008), is a 43-item scale based entirely on Loehr's (1986) definition of mental toughness. Items are scored on a 7-point Likert scale and include: "negative emotions are hard to change", "competitive circumstances affect me", "I display confidence/energy", and "I compete fully recovered". Preliminary Rasch analysis demonstrated a good model-data fit (Mack & Ragan). However, the sample of 261 undergraduate students is below the recommended minimum for such analysis (Tabachnick & Fidell, 2007). In addition, there remains ambiguity as to whom the inventory is targeting. Mack and Ragan intimate that though the instrument is of "great interest to those helping individuals perform and comply with rehabilitation", future researchers ought to focus on "developing more specific items that are tailored to the early stages of rehabilitation to better measure and ultimately serve our patients" (p. 131). The authors need to state clearly whether the MeBTough is an inventory designed solely to measure mental toughness in injury rehabilitation contexts. Moreover, irrespective of context, the instrument needs to be subjected to thorough exploratory and confirmatory analysis techniques before it can be recommended as an index for assessing mental toughness.

Loehr's blueprint revisited

The Psychological Performance Inventory

The above findings reflect the difficulties researchers have encountered in their endeavours to construct a psychometrically sound measurement of mental toughness. As evidenced by the aforementioned efforts of Mack and Ragan (2008), particularly influential in the area of mental toughness research is Jim Loehr's (1986) frequently cited monograph, *Mental toughness training for sports: Achieving athletic excellence*, and his Psychological Performance Inventory (PPI). However, despite its ongoing influence on research and practice, minimal rigorous evaluation has been conducted on the psychometric properties of the PPI. In trying to define mental toughness, Loehr interviewed hundreds of athletes who gave surprisingly similar accounts of their experiences prior to and during peak performance.

Personality characteristics such as a high level of resolution, a refusal to be intimidated, an ability to stay focused, a capacity for retaining an optimum level of arousal, an eagerness to compete, an unyielding attitude when being beaten, and an inflexible insistence on finishing a contest rather than conceding defeat emerged from the interviews. Subsequent analysis yielded seven subscales of mental toughness; namely, self-confidence, negative energy control, attention control, visualization and imagery control, motivation, positive energy, and attitude control. The resultant PPI was one of the first instruments to include specific cognitive-behavioural and self-evaluation dimensions.

The inventory was developed to assess "mental strengths and weaknesses" (Loehr, 1986, p. 157) and to improve athletes' awareness and understanding of their mental skills. Although Loehr offered a persuasive discussion of the instrument and the rationale for its seven subscales, the conceptual and theoretical basis for the instrument was not strong and, in particular, he presented no psychometric support for its use. In fact, though the PPI is a promising tool for use in the assessment and potential development of mental toughness and continues to be used in research (e.g., T. W. Allen, 1988; Dongsung & Kang-Heon, 1994; Hanrahan, Grove, & Lockwood, 1990; Kang-Heon, Dongsung, Myung-Woo, & Elisa, 1994; Kuan & Roy, 2007), to date, only limited research has been conducted on its reliability and validity.

Psychometric analyses of the PPI

To date, there are only two published studies which have examined the psychometric properties of Loehr's (1986) PPI (namely, Golby, Sheard, & van Wersch, 2007; Middleton et al., 2004c). Neither study found support for the instrument's structural validity using exploratory (Golby et al.), or confirmatory (Middleton et al.), techniques. However, the Middleton et al. study recruited fewer participants ($N = 263$) than are generally recommended for factor analysis (Tabachnick & Fidell, 2007). Indeed, the sample size used in their study could only be described as "fair" (Comrey & Lee, 1992). Further, and potentially problematic with regard to external validity, was the young mean age of the participants (14 years); Golby et al. recruited 408 sport performers with a mean age of 24 years.

Construction of a revised model

The alternative 5-factor 16-item mental toughness structure suggested by Middleton et al. (2004c) did not include a measure of self-confidence or an appealing measure of control, two mental toughness characteristics identified in earlier chapters. Therefore, Golby et al. (2007) extended Middleton et al.'s earlier psychometric work on the PPI by successfully developing a multidimensional questionnaire designed to assess mental toughness in the athletic domain. From their exploratory analysis of the PPI, Golby et al. ultimately yielded four factors of mental toughness; these were labelled determination, self-belief, positive cognition, and visualization. The revised instrument was named the PPI-A. Additional analyses beyond those conducted by Middleton et al. were used to investigate the factor structure of the PPI-A. Crucially, Golby et al. were the first researchers into a psychometrically acceptable measure of mental toughness to employ the Schmid–Leiman procedure (Schmid & Leiman, 1957) for the purpose of conducting higher-order factor analysis. Schmid–Leiman results suggested evidence of both a general mental toughness factor, as well as the four previously mentioned first-order factors. Finally, model fit was assessed using confirmatory factor analysis, and both absolute and incremental fit indices showed good support for the correlated 4-factor PPI-A model. The PPI-A inventory is shown in Table 4.2.

A potential limitation of the 4-factor PPI-A is that it does not include a measure of control, a characteristic routinely identified in the mental toughness literature (cf. Clough et al., 2002; G. Jones

Table 4.2 PPI-A: Item number and content

No. Content for mental toughness items by subscale

Determination
1　The goals I've set for myself as a player keep me working hard
2　I don't have to be pushed to play or practise hard. I am my own best igniter
3　I'm willing to give whatever it takes to reach my full potential as a player

Self-belief
4　I lose my confidence very quickly
5　I can keep strong positive emotion flowing during competition
6　I am a positive thinker during competition
7　My self-talk during competition is negative

Positive cognition
8　I can clear interfering emotion quickly and regain my focus
9　Playing this sport gives me a genuine sense of joy and fulfilment
10　I can change negative moods into positive ones by controlling my thinking
11　I can turn crisis into opportunity

Visualization
12　I mentally practise my physical skills
13　Thinking in pictures about my sport comes easy for me
14　I visualize working through tough situations prior to competition

Source: Adapted from Golby et al. (2007).

et al., 2002; Thelwell et al., 2005). The original PPI negative energy control and attention control subscales were structurally weak, and, as a result of rigorous exploratory analysis in the Golby et al. (2007) study, did not have a sufficient number of items for confirmatory factor analysis. Given that good attentional control is inextricably linked with good emotional control (Thomas, Murphy, & Hardy, 1999), the next stage was to develop a scale that includes a *control* subscale capable of measuring athletes' anxiety and coping response.

Development of the Sports Mental Toughness Questionnaire

Sheard, Golby, and van Wersch (2009) have developed the first psychometrically acceptable measure of mental toughness (namely, the Sports Mental Toughness Questionnaire; SMTQ) that includes a *control* subscale. To begin the process of construct validation, the authors of the scale used the raw data themes and quotes from qualitative studies (e.g., Bull et al., 2005; Clough et al., 2002; Fourie & Potgieter, 2001; Gould et al., 2002; G. Jones et al., 2002; Loehr, 1986; Thelwell et al., 2005) to develop a corpus of sport-relevant items. An initial pool of 53 items was administered to five female and five male athletes, and to 10 coaches working in a variety of sports. This panel of experts assessed the initial 53-item pool for comprehensibility by athletes. Using a dichotomous scale (applicable vs. inapplicable), they were instructed to assess the applicability of each item in their respective sport. Using the ratings provided by athletes and coaches, and on their numerous comments, several items were re-written in order to improve their clarity and to broaden their applicability across sports, thus establishing good content validity. Experts involved in previous mental toughness investigations reviewed the resulting bank of items. They retained 18 items.

The second stage of construct validation involved 633 performers, with a mean age of 22 years, drawn from 25 sport classifications, and competing at international, national, county and provincial, or club and regional standards, completing the SMTQ during training camps. Principal axis factoring analysis yielded a 3-factor 14-item model, which explained 40.7 per cent of the variance. The factors correspond meaningfully with the definitions of mental toughness within the extant literature: confidence (vs. self-doubt), constancy (vs. irresolute), and control (vs. agitation) are themes, as we have seen, encountered frequently in recent qualitative studies (cf. Bull et al., 2005; Clough et al., 2002; Gould et al., 2002; G. Jones et al., 2002; Thelwell et al., 2005), and Loehr's (1986) mental toughness blueprint. Moreover, the SMTQ is the only psychometrically acceptable mental toughness instrument that includes a measure of emotional and negative energy control.

The third construct validation stage involved using an independent sample of 509 athletes, with a mean age of 20 years, competing at the aforementioned standards, and representative of 26 sports, to complete the 3-factor 14-item SMTQ. A single factor underlying mental toughness (G_{MT}) was identified with higher-order exploratory factor analysis using the Schmid–Leiman procedure. Further, the three factors extracted in the exploratory analysis exhibited good internal consistency with each independent sample used in this study ($\alpha \geq .70$; Kline, 2005): Study 1: Confidence = .80; Constancy = .74; Control = .71; Study 2: Confidence = .79; Constancy = .76; Control = .72).

Confirmatory analysis using structural equation modelling confirmed the overall structure of the SMTQ. The oblique 3-factor model yielded absolute fit indices that indicated a good model fit: χ^2 (74, N = 509) = 182.56, $p < .01$, χ^2/df = 2.47, goodness-of-fit index (GFI) = .95, adjusted goodness-of-fit index (AGFI) = .93, root mean square error of approximation (RMSEA) = .05, root mean square residual (RMR) = .05. Similarly, the incremental fit indices indicated good support for the model: Tucker-Lewis Index (TLI) = .91, comparative fit index (CFI) = .92, incremental fit index (IFI) = .93. Divergent validity was demonstrated by the observed pattern of weak to moderate correlations between the SMTQ and the hardiness Personal Views Survey III-R (PVS III-R) (Maddi & Khoshaba, 2001; r range = .14 to .33), dispositional optimism Revised Life Orientation Test (LOT-R) (Scheier, Carver, & Bridges, 1994; r range = .23 to .38), and affect Positive Affect and Negative Affect Schedule (PANAS) (Watson, Clark, & Tellegen, 1988; r range = .12 to .49) subscales.

Finally, subgroup differences relative to competitive standard, gender, and age indicated some variation in mental toughness levels, revealing that the SMTQ possesses good discriminative power. The implication of these findings is that, first, and subject to further validation, different sets of norms may need to be developed. And second, in addition to the many attributes requisite to outstanding sport performance, a psychological profile that includes high levels of mental toughness appeared to distinguish older, male performers operating at the highest competitive standard (i.e., international) (Sheard et al., 2009). The SMTQ is presented in Table 4.3.

Rationale for the SMTQ subscales

Confidence

That six items loaded on the SMTQ confidence subscale, and explained most of the scale's variance in its development,

Table 4.3 SMTQ item wording

No.	Content for mental toughness items by subscale

Confidence
1   I interpret potential threats as positive opportunities
2   I have an unshakeable confidence in my ability
3   I have qualities that set me apart from other competitors
4   I have what it takes to perform well while under pressure
5   Under pressure, I am able to make decisions with confidence and commitment
6   I can regain my composure if I have momentarily lost it

Constancy
7   I am committed to completing the tasks I have to do
8   I take responsibility for setting myself challenging targets
9   I give up in difficult situations
10   I get distracted easily and lose my concentration

Control
11   I worry about performing poorly
12   I am overcome by self-doubt
13   I get anxious by events I did not expect or cannot control
14   I get angry and frustrated when things do not go my way

Source: Adapted from Sheard et al. (2009)

corroborates the findings of previous research (Gucciardi et al., 2008; G. Jones et al., 2002; Thelwell et al., 2005), which reported the emergence of high self-confidence and self-belief as the most important attribute of mentally tough performers. The six items in this subscale stress the importance of athletes having belief in their ability to achieve their goals and believing that they are different to and, crucially, better than their opponents. SMTQ confidence comprised items tapping similar self-regulatory feelings such as self-belief and staying positive, especially when facing challenging and pressured situations, as highly competitive sport often presents. SMTQ confidence reflects self-efficacy theory in that the subscale is concerned with the independent effects of positive self-perception on real-life outcomes, irrespective of performers' "actual" competence. Thus, as constitutive of mental toughness, confidence is considered a cause, rather than a consequence, of high performance. As Tomas Chamorro-Premuzic and Adrian Furnham stated:

"The idea that confidence may affect an individual's performance has existed so long that it seems irrelevant to date it" (Chamorro-Premuzic & Furnham, 2006, p. 769). There is a substantial theoretical overlap between the concept of confidence and self-efficacy, notably the emphasis on the self-fulfilling effects of subjective evaluations – regardless of their accuracy – as determinants of actual performance. As the incomparable Muhammad Ali said: "I am a great golfer, I just haven't played the game yet" (as cited in Goodbody, 2002, p. 32). Unshakeable self-belief!

Constancy

This factor reflects athletes' determination to meet the demands of training and competition, willingness to take responsibility for setting training and competition goals, possession of an unyielding attitude, and an ability to concentrate. Mentally tough performers recognize that they must take responsibility for their training and competition performances. They recognize also that, ultimately, in performance, they are on their own. Implicit in SMTQ constancy is the assumption that without ownership there is no responsibility.

SMTQ constancy also taps into athletes' preparedness to focus, to show grit, and to not give up in the face of adversity. These items reflect the association between successful athletes' tendency to keep a more task-oriented focus of concentration and avoid preoccupation with negative outcomes, which may otherwise increase the likelihood of reducing effort or even quitting (J. M. Williams & Krane, 2001). This very much reflects the mental toughness described by former Australian cricket captain Steve Waugh who stated that: "The arts of concentration and discipline were a part of my game. These two attributes form the nucleus of mental toughness" (Waugh, 2006, pp. 23–24). Athletes scoring highly in constancy are predicted to be more likely to be able to maintain their focus, particularly when faced with provocation. The deliberate mental disintegration tactic of "sledging" (i.e., verbally abusing and insulting opponents) has, sadly, become widespread in sport, most notably cricket (Barnes, 2008a, 2008b, 2008f). Banter is fine; sledging is offensive and unacceptable. Mentally tough athletes high in constancy cope with intimidating bitter invective hurled their way. Moreover, mentally tough sportspeople have no need of it in the first place.

Control

Perceived control, the perception that one can bring about a desired outcome, is regarded by some as a fundamental human need and a central component of psychological health. People who believe they have control over events in their lives feel better about themselves, cope better with adversity and life crises, and perform better on various cognitive tasks, as compared to those who have less feeling of control. The notion of perceived control is reflected in various theoretical constructs, such as locus of control (Rotter, 1954), health locus of control (Wallston, 1989), self-efficacy (Bandura, 1997), and hardiness (Kobasa, 1979).

SMTQ control addresses the omission of a similar subscale in the PPI-A, the only other published psychometrically acceptable measure of mental toughness. Keeping emotions in control and remaining calm and relaxed under pressured situations (Côté, 2001), plus a capacity to regain psychological control following unexpected, uncontrollable events (G. Jones et al., 2002), are consistently reported attributes of mental toughness. The adverse repercussions of failing to do this in both individual (see Sheard, 2003) and team (see Greenwood, 2009) sports are well documented.

Recent developments

Sheard (2008b) extended previous psychometric work on the PPI-A and the SMTQ. A sample of 455 athletes, with a mean age of 22 years and drawn from 19 sport classifications, completed both inventories. Higher-order factor analyses suggested evidence of a G_{MT} factor in each scale, as well as their respective first-order factors. Absolute and incremental confirmatory factor analysis fit indices showed good support for each model. All factors in each scale showed good reliability. Divergent validity was established by a pattern of correlations between each mental toughness scale and positive psychological measures. Finally, further evidence of each scale's discriminative power was observed; specifically, international-level competitors were characterized by the highest levels of mental toughness when adjustments were made for age, sport type (i.e., individual, team), sport category (i.e., contact or non-contact), and gender covariates.

The work of Sheard and co-workers offers support for the PPI-A and SMTQ as valid measures of mental toughness. The instruments possess encouraging psychometric integrity. In particular, recent research with full-time professional elite-level rugby league referees suggests that each scale is sufficiently sensitive to detect changes in levels of mental toughness (Sheard & Golby, 2008). As construct validation is an ongoing process (Marsh, 1997), further meaningful comparisons should now be made on PPI-A and SMTQ data collected over time, with the recommendation that practitioners use changes in PPI-A and SMTQ scores as indices for evaluating the impact of psychological skills training. This would fulfil the ultimate construct validation criterion of application in research and practice.

Conclusion

At long last, after much conceptual debate, researchers have finally developed psychometrically acceptable multi-factorial measures of mental toughness; namely, the PPI-A and the SMTQ. Each is a concise 14-item scale that clearly taps into the very characteristics that have been routinely identified in the qualitative literature. Collectively, satisfying confirmatory factor analysis absolute and incremental fit index benchmarks, each has shown good psychometric properties. Rigorous psychometric testing has revealed promising features of the PPI-A and the SMTQ, lending support to the instruments' factorial validity, reliability, and differential validity. Ultimately, the PPI-A and the SMTQ are the only published mental toughness questionnaires that have been subjected to rigorous exploratory and confirmatory analysis techniques, and have demonstrated acceptable psychometric properties.

Mindful that construct validation is an ongoing process, a number of research projects are in progress using the PPI-A and the SMTQ with performers, coaches, and officials across a diverse range of sports. Particularly noteworthy, in collaboration with researchers around the world, work has begun on the translation of each scale into different languages, notably French, German, Japanese, Portuguese, and Turkish. These studies of further validation will enhance the efficacy of each scale in practical and research settings. The PPI-A and the SMTQ are strongly advocated as valuable research tools for use in psychological interventions.

It is clear from the first four chapters of this book that the mentally tough athlete possesses, and, crucially, can be measured in, determination/constancy, self-belief/confidence, positive thinking (especially in difficult situations), visualization, and anxiety/emotional control. In view of the breadth of characteristics encapsulated in the mental toughness mindset, it might be, as Gaudreau and Blondin (2002) reported of athletes' use of coping strategies in sport, that, because of their situation-driven nature and multiple determinants, mental toughness characteristics serve different functions for different individuals in different competitive situations. Mentally tough performers are able to call on these attributes, whether singly or in combination, when faced with the appropriate circumstance. However, their ability to do this cannot be wholly innate. Therefore, it must be learnt. The next chapter addresses the question: How is the mentally tough mindset developed?

5   Developing and maintaining mental toughness

We need courage for the most strange, the most singular, and the most inexplicable that we may encounter.

Rainer Maria Rilke

Introduction

We live in pressured, stressful times. Whether living through this period is any more stressful for us than experiencing the Industrial Revolution or either of the last century's World Wars was for previous generations is highly debatable. The challenges today's sports stars face are slight compared with those of, for example, the legendary Australian cricketer Keith Miller who famously remarked: "When athletes nowadays talk of pressure they only reveal what they don't know of life" (as cited in Parkinson, 2004, p. 8). Miller had plenty to talk about and his approach to cricket, as well as life, was shaped during the Second World War, when he flew fighter planes over Britain for the Royal Australian Air Force. Having come through such a terrifying experience it is easy to understand why he felt there was more to life than cricket. Indeed, he had the perfect answer when asked if he ever felt under pressure on the cricket field: "Pressure, I'll tell you what pressure is. Pressure is a Messerschmitt up your arse, playing cricket is not" (as cited in Fraser, 2004, p. 58). If only we could have measured his level of mental toughness!

Nowadays, I believe most of us would agree that, largely due to the exponential advancement in communication technologies, the "instant-everything culture" is omnipresent. The benefit of this advance is our tremendous capability, but the trade-off is an escapable pressure to keep up with continual developments. Moreover, instant success, instant results, and, in some cases, instant fame have fuelled a belief in the possibility of achievement with little effort and exacerbated the cult of celebrity and shallow fame. This is particularly prevalent in sport. For example, there is an argument that many performers are "given" far too much too early in their careers, that they have not yet worked hard enough to have earned the right to such accolades. Indeed, this is the view of veteran Chelsea and England football player Frank Lampard (more than 70 international appearances), who has been critical of the unwarranted comfort zone and easy lifestyles afforded many young footballers (as cited by Winter, 2009). Particularly resonant is that they have yet to achieve anything in their sports, they have merely got a step on the learning curve. And that is the point: a *learning* curve. Just as athletes learn the physical, physiological, mechanical, technical, and tactical components of their sports, so they must devote significant time to their psychological development. The "finished article" is not born; it must be developed and maintained.

Owners and their teams of coaches must be prepared to invest time and money into the development of their athletes. The right culture must be created, if otherwise talented individuals are not to let themselves down (see Harman, 2008; Hodgkinson, 2008). Moreover, athletes themselves must recognize this, and practise patience in regard to the development of their sporting abilities. In addition, the mentally tough mindset must be nurtured. It is increasingly recognized also by governing bodies of sports that, just as there is a need to develop technical and physical competence, there is an additional requirement to develop the necessary mental attributes. For example, the British Equestrian Federation has identified the development of mental toughness in its athletes as crucial to the success of its "Long Term Rider Development" programme (C. Wilson, Edwards, & Collins, 2005).

Sport performers need to develop the mindset that affords them the opportunities to meet a challenge and to overcome the difficulties that obstruct their progress (Kuehl, Kuehl, & Tefertiller,

2005). They must have resolve, dedication, courage, and persever-ance to increase the likelihood of achieving success. This begins with the "right" attitude; put simply, athletes must train and compete having accepted personal responsibility for doing everything within their control to optimize their performance. Within their control are strategies such as positive affirmations, making practice and com-petition behaviours routine, learning to let go of mistakes, and even looking at failure as a stepping stone to future achievement. These behaviours reflect the mentally tough mindset and make it far more likely that such performers will "step up" successfully.

To demonstrate the point, mental toughness attributes (namely, self-confidence, coping with adversity, activation control) distin-guished top-ranked under-19 rugby union players from their lower-ranked counterparts (Andrew, Grobbelaar, & Potgieter, 2007). Similarly, professional rugby league footballers operating at the highest level (i.e., international) possess significantly higher levels of mental toughness than their sub-elite counterparts (Golby & Sheard, 2004). If, as Vince Lombardi said: "mental toughness is an essential key to success" (as cited in Cadigan, 2008), the likeli-hood of sporting success is, at least to some extent, dependent on a mentally tough mindset. We can also assume that international-level performers were not as mentally tough in the early stages of their career. Rather, they developed the requisite mental toughness characteristics that contributed to their progression to the sporting summit.

The essentials

Athletes' development of their mental toughness is predicated on the supposition that rational thought processes and self-discipline take precedence over emotional reactions. According to Scarnati (2000), enormous self-discipline and willpower are required. Scarnati's essentials for developing mental toughness require indi-viduals to: develop competence; do the "right" thing; develop the spiritual as well as the physical you; stay steady, resist pressure, and do quality work; develop a positive sense of worth and self-confidence; conquer emotions with rational thinking; develop persistence and resolve when facing problems; develop career goals;

learn to say "no"; and never empower or enable others to mentally cripple you (pp. 174–175). Similar attributes were assessed by Marchant et al. (2007) who, from their research of managers in the workplace, concluded that mental toughness has a state tendency, suggesting it has the potential to be trained, and develop with age and managerial responsibilities.

A long-term process

It would be unrealistic to expect the mentally tough performer to possess characteristics, such as those mentioned by Scarnati (2000) above, without proceeding through developmental stages. Athletes, coaches, and parents need to realize that, like physical and technical skills, the development of mental toughness requires time and practice. To expect immediate success is to misunderstand the desired enduring effect of mental skills adoption. Dan Gould and co-workers found that mental skills of the elite develop over extended periods of time and are influenced by a wide range of individuals (e.g., teachers, parents, coaches) (Gould et al., 2002). In this vein, Declan Connaughton and colleagues conducted a study with regard to the development of mental toughness and whether it requires maintenance (Connaughton et al., 2008). Seven of the samples used originally by G. Jones et al. (2002) participated in semi-structured interviews. Findings indicated that the development of mental toughness is a long-term process that encompasses a multitude of underlying mechanisms that operate in a combined, rather than independent, fashion.

Reflecting Bloom's (1985) three career phases (namely, early, middle, and later years), participants in the Connaughton et al. (2008) study perceived mental toughness to develop in stages. In the early years, the experience of critical incidents was felt to have a powerful influence in cultivating mental toughness. The athletes' motivational climate should be challenging, rewarding, and enjoyable. This remained important in the middle and later years, but these subsequent stages were also reported to provide their own unique impression in the development of mental toughness. This suggestion corroborates the finding of Thelwell et al. (2005), whose professional football participants attached importance to their environment and experience during their formative years in regard to the development of their mental toughness. In particular, parental influence, childhood background, and transition into an appropriate cricket environment were found to be key environmental influences in the development of mental toughness in international cricketers (Bull et al., 2005).

The middle years were more competitive for performers in the Connaughton et al. (2008) study. Opportunities existed for athletes to learn from significant others (e.g., senior athletes, coaches, parents) and to have a heightened determination to succeed.

The later years were alleged to develop mental toughness fully through increased competitive experience and the use of basic and advanced psychological skills and strategies. Bull et al. (2005) suggest that more attention should be devoted to creating tough environments so that participants can learn from their experiences, rather than spending time on formal mental skills training. However, much further empirical work is needed to substantiate the claim. An interesting point in the Bull et al. study was that mentally tough performers reported a sense of being an outsider (i.e., playing cricket in a foreign country) as being important in developing mental toughness.

It was also reported by Connaughton et al. (2008) that once mental toughness had been developed, three perceived underlying mechanisms were required to maintain this mindset; namely, a desire and motivation to succeed that was insatiable and internalized; a support network that included sporting and non-sporting personnel; and the effective use of basic and advanced psychological skills. We have already covered desire and motivation as constituent characteristics of mental toughness. The benefits of a support network of significant others are well established in the literature (see Pargman, 1999; Ray & Wiese-Bjornstal, 1999). We shall draw our attention to the third of Connaughton et al.'s underlying mechanisms – the effective use of psychological skills.

Psychological skills training

In their aforementioned examination of the development and maintenance of mental toughness, Connaughton et al. (2008) indicated the use of psychological skills training (PST) to be critical for both aspects. Encouraging athletes to use psychological skills during their formative years may promote, for example, better coping skills once they mature (Lane, Harwood, Terry, & Karageorghis, 2004). Well-planned PST programmes are an opportunity to nurture positively young athletes' personal development in competitive sport and to facilitate their growth in other areas of their life by generalizing the use of mental skills (Tremayne & Tremayne, 2004). However, despite a wealth of literature citing the benefits of PST programme interventions, few studies have measured mental toughness empirically as a specific dependent variable.

Notably, Sheard and Golby (2006a) reported a significant ($p <$ .01) improvement in levels of mental toughness among a group of 36 national-level swimmers following a 7-week PST programme. The majority of participants ($n = 28$) improved their mental toughness scores post-intervention having been exposed to a programme of goal setting, visualization, relaxation, concentration, and thought stopping skills. Interestingly, reflective that mental toughness is related to general well-being as well as performance, all participants reported the PST intervention as useful and that they would continue to practise the skills contained within the programme for competitive performance and life in general. In particular, the swimmers expressed how the skills learned in the PST programme had benefited other areas of their lives (e.g., school, college, relationships).

It has been suggested that athletes may neglect PST due to their perception that attributes such as mental toughness are inherent rather than developed (Lane, 2008). Sport psychologists need to work with coaches to counter this misunderstanding. This is particularly important in light of recent research findings that more than a quarter of sampled young provincial-level South African netball players indicated average, below average, or poor psychological preparation for competitions (Van den Heever, Grobbelaar, & Potgieter, 2007).

A criticism levelled at some intervention programmes has been that they were not designed to examine mental toughness; rather, they were designed as practical approaches, promoting specific mental skills in order to overcome adversity and improve performance (Connaughton et al., 2008). However, many of the PST techniques advocated by, for example, Jim Loehr (1986) and Alan Goldberg (1998) have been supported empirically. Significant improvements in mental toughness and swimming performance followed PST interventions underpinned by Loehr and Goldberg's work (see Sheard & Golby, 2006a). Other research has demonstrated the positive effects of visualization on other outcome variables, which, as covered in earlier chapters, are conceptually constitutive of mental toughness; for example, self-confidence (Garza & Feltz, 1998), self-efficacy (Carboni, Burke, Joyner, Hardy, & Blom, 2002), and decreased anxiety (Vadocz, Hall, & Moritz, 1997).

Particularly noteworthy is the observation that the most successful PST programmes are those in which sessions are conducted on an individual basis. Participants mentioned this during the social validation component of the Sheard and Golby (2006a) swimming study. Interestingly, Puni (1963) stressed that such psychological preparation for a competition must be individualized and that it be based on the athlete's idiosyncrasies (e.g., temperament, character, motivation, and abilities). Individualization is a must in team sports as well as individual sports. However, in team sports, individual preparation should be conducted in the context of psychological preparation of the team as a whole.

A force for good in injury rehabilitation?

Returning to sport following a serious injury can be a stressful process for athletes (Bianco, 2001). Returning athletes often experience fears associated with re-injury (Kvist, Ek, Sporrstedt, & Good, 2005), concerns about their ability to perform up to pre-injury levels (Crossman, 1997), and pressures to meet specific return deadlines (Bianco, 2001). In addition, the role of the coach is critical. Good coaches will possess a thorough understanding of the stressors (e.g., physical, social, performance) of returning to sport and recognizing the importance of assisting athletes with this transition (Podlog & Eklund, 2007).

If athletes have high mental toughness in the domain of their sport, does this mindset transfer to other fields? Though Sheard and Golby (2006a) showed the transference to different situations of the ameliorative effects of increased mental toughness, high levels of mental toughness in one activity domain are not necessarily accompanied by high mental toughness in other spheres of activity (or inactivity). For example, what does mentally tough mean or involve to an athlete who is severely injured? The answer could be different than what it means to a performer who is fully fit and focused on other performance criteria. Mental toughness may need to be developed to improve injury rehabilitation outcome probabilities, as well as the more obvious ameliorative effects in training and competition performance.

In the domain of sport injuries, mental toughness may be justifiably associated with pain tolerance. Throughout their careers, many sport performers are confronted with various situations in which the ability to tolerate pain is extremely important. Moreover, athletes with a high level of pain tolerance are expected to achieve a higher level of performance than performers with low levels of pain tolerance (Whitmarsh & Alderman, 1993). For example, in winning the 2008 US Open Golf Championship despite excruciating pain, and claiming his 14th major title, it was reported that Tiger Woods "displayed tremendous mental toughness" (Elliott, 2008, p. 9).

One recent study found that elite swimmers high in mental toughness reported fewer injuries than less mentally tough individuals competing at the same level (Levy, Clough, Polman, Marchant, & Earle, 2005). The same team of researchers investigated the relationship between mental toughness, sport injury beliefs, pain, and adherence toward a sport injury rehabilitation programme. Using a sample of 70 patients undertaking a sport injury rehabilitation programme for a tendonitis-related injury, they found that high mentally tough individuals displayed more positive threat appraisals and were better able to cope with pain than their less mentally tough counterparts (Levy, Polman, Clough, Marchant, & Earle, 2006). The authors also reported a greater attendance at rehabilitation sessions by more mentally tough individuals. However, more positive behaviour during clinic rehabilitation was characterized by low mental toughness. Levy et al. (2006) suggested that this might be due to "high mentally tough individuals appraising their injury to be less severe and less susceptible to reoccur and thereby perceive compliance to clinic based activity to be less important" (p. 252). Thus, despite the benefits of being mentally tough, a high degree of mental toughness may have negative consequences upon rehabilitation behaviour and, subsequently, recovery outcomes. Though it would appear that they probably cope better and process pain more effectively, injured performers high in mental toughness could also return prematurely to training or competition. Clearly, there is a need for athletes to develop the appropriate mental toughness attributes to deal more effectively with injury and rehabilitation.

Mental toughness as conceptualized by Sheard et al. (2009) would predict adherence to clear plans and goals of a programme of injury rehabilitation. Mentally tough athletes would have clear goals and even clearer restrictions. Such performers would also not use injury as a displacement for poor performance. They will reject the notion that they are merely passive recipients of care; rather, they will demonstrate an active engagement with regard to their rehabilitation programme. Mental toughness ought to increase the likelihood of collaboration, commitment, responsibility, and ownership with regard to any injury rehabilitation programme. High mentally tough performers will move away from the culture of "no pain, no gain". For such athletes it will be a case of the appropriate pain for the right amount of gain. I suggest that it takes more mental toughness to say "I'm not ready", than to jump in too soon and conform to pressure from any prevailing "sport ethic" environment (R. H. Hughes & Coakley, 1991). Such a mindset will also assist injured athletes to maintain their mental toughness post-rehabilitation.

Further, there is no reason why the very skills used in PST programmes to enhance training and competition performance should not be used to achieve the aforementioned mental toughness objectives as an integral part of injury rehabilitation programmes. For example, motivational mastery imagery (Hardy, Gammage, & Hall, 2001), and motivational imagery for goal setting (Driediger, Hall, & Callow, 2006), in particular, have been found to improve injured athletes' levels of mental toughness.

Goal setting is also an essential part of any injury rehabilitation programme. Goals need to be specific, measurable, and most of all, achievable. Danish and colleagues (Danish, Petitpas, & Hale, 1993) described an educational-developmental model in which injury is not seen as a problem, but as an opportunity for growth and development in and outside of sport. Recent research findings also suggest that mental toughness may have implications for the personal growth and development of athletes in response to adversity in sport, such as injury and rehabilitation (Galli & Vealey, 2008). Perhaps mentally tough performers are more likely to respond to injury and rehabilitation in a way that allows them to achieve personal growth.

One world champion performer who has had more than his fair share of injury setbacks advocates just such a philosophy. England rugby union World Cup winner Jonny Wilkinson wrote of his reaction after injuring knee ligaments at the beginning of the domestic season in September 2006: "It doesn't take me long, even from the biggest setbacks, to return to my core belief in sport and in life, too. If you want something enough and if it's worth enough to you, then you have to fight, fight, fight and then fight some more. I don't mean physically attacking other people, I mean smashing through challenges, I mean standing tall and believing in myself when others stop doing so. It entails getting up as soon as I physically can after I get knocked down and digging my heels in when it gets too tough for others. It is not time to call it a day until I decide I want to do so" (J. Wilkinson, 2008, pp. 247–248).

Two months after he had rehabilitated from that injury, Wilkinson sustained a serious kidney injury. Recollecting this time in his autobiography, his mentally tough philosophy is even more apparent: "When one door closes, another one opens. For the first time since the serious neck injury, which seemed to kick off this bizarre run of setbacks, I considered just how fragile my body (and the human body in general) was. It reinforced my growing under-standing that our true strength and power must lie inside rather than in the muscles we build" (J. Wilkinson, 2008, p. 256). These recollections reveal a mentally tough competitor who has had to come to terms with continual injury setbacks as a postscript to World Cup glory.

A final thought on sport injury rehabilitation and mental toughness. Given the perception within the elite sporting community, and society in general, that elite athletes are motivated to use performance-enhancing drugs, an interesting line of enquiry for future research in the domain of sport injuries would be the relationship between mental toughness and the use of performance-enhancing drugs for rehabilitation purposes. A recent study reported that 50 per cent of its sample of 116 elite Australian Rules footballers and soccer players indicated a high likelihood that they would use a performance-enhancing drug for rehabilitation purposes (Strelan & Boeckmann, 2006). The athletes believed that the use of a banned harmful substance was a viable response to a career-threatening situation, and many indicated their willingness to use such drugs if faced with such a threat. It would be interesting to discover if such a belief corresponded with high or low mental toughness.

Coaches' responsibilities for developing athletes' mental toughness

Of the themes to emerge from a recent study of elite coaches' views on effective talent development (Martindale, Collins, & Abraham, 2007), two were particularly prominent: recognizing that "mental toughness is the key to progression" and that athletes must possess the "mental desire and attitude to improve/succeed". To this end, coaches have a responsibility to model and teach the concepts of mental toughness in the pursuit of sporting excellence. In addition to the attributes identified and discussed previously, other desirable attributes include sportsmanship, fair play, and respect for opponents. Coaches need to teach young athletes, in particular, how to behave and conduct themselves properly. Above all, this needs to be conducted in an environment of open and honest communication.

The overall goal of any coach is the development of the athlete (Côté, Salmela, Trudel, Baria, & Russell, 1995). Of the four higher-order categories identified in a recent study for building a successful sport programme, "individual growth" was considered particularly important (Vallée & Bloom, 2005). The study's expert coaches aimed at developing performers into high-level athletes, instilling intrinsic motivation to maximize their potential. Fostering individual growth was accomplished through life skills development and empowerment of each athlete.

As one coach in the Vallée and Bloom (2005) study put it: "Being a champion is in every part of their life, including how they carry themselves. It affects those decisions they make around eating, sleeping, and hydrating. It is that whole package" (pp. 187–188). All coaches mentioned positive reinforcement and persuasion as indispensable tactics to enhance self-confidence in their players. Reflecting this, another coach added: "I think your players very much reflect your attitude as a coach. If someone ever mentioned anything about not being as good as or at a lower level, that was unacceptable. We spoke of ourselves as winners, as successful women, who would have no reason to look back at ourselves. We did everything that we could to give ourselves an opportunity to be successful" (p. 188).

All coaches in the Vallée and Bloom (2005) study stated that their ultimate philosophy included more than winning games (see Chapter 1). It involved developing well-rounded individuals who would be successful in life. One coach even explicitly stated that winning the national championship was not the end goal; rather, it was to teach her athletes about life through sport. Clearly, this coach recognizes the tremendous opportunity that exists to shape young people and to have a positive influence on their lives.

Challenging experiences

There is a widespread cultural assumption that controlled exposure to challenge can be potentially beneficial (Miles & Priest, 1990; Watts, Webster, Morley, & Cohen, 1992). For example, adventure experiences have gained an enduring reputation for developing desirable personality characteristics in its participants that reflect the currency of mental toughness. Such experiences as rock climbing, canoeing, orienteering, and camping have long been suggested to foster qualities such as initiative, perseverance, determination, self-restraint, co-operation, and resourcefulness (Celebi & Ozen, 2004; Luckner & Nadler, 1997; Schoel, Prouty, & Radcliffe, 1988).

The notion of adventure experiences assisting in the development of mental toughness is intuitively appealing. This is particularly emphasized if the theoretical rationale adopts a "neo-Hahnian approach"; that is, that adventure experiences build character or have certain therapeutic effects associated with personal charac-teristics (Brookes, 2003). This approach represents a development-by-challenge philosophy and provides an underlying justification for adventure experiences (Neill & Dias, 2001). A general and a research-based literature exist on the character-building effects of, for example, Outward Bound, outdoor adventure courses, and outdoor adventure education curriculum activities (e.g., Bronson, Gibson, Kichar, & Priest, 1992; Cason & Gillis, 1994; Hattie, Marsh, Neill, & Richards, 1997; McKenzie, 2000; Neill & Dias, 2001; Sheard & Golby, 2006b).

Adventure experiences can be used as an effective medium for participants to recognize and to understand their own weaknesses, strengths, and personal resources (Nadler, 1993; Taniguchi & Freeman, 2004). Moreover, the skills learned in challenging situ-ations are deemed to be transferable (Priest & Gass, 2005). Adventure experiences have a major enduring impact on the lives, in general, and the psychological development, in particular, of participants. Evidence suggests that the experiences provided by adventure experiences contribute to improvements in self-esteem, self-confidence, locus of control, conflict resolution, problem-solving skills, and group cohesion (Cason & Gillis, 1994; Hans, 2000; Hattie et al., 1997; Neill & Richards, 1998).

Climbing Mount Everest

Psychologist David Fletcher provided scientific support for a group of mountaineers on Everest Base Camp in April 2007. Rather than merely coping with the pressure, the trekkers and climbers had to develop the qualities that would enable them to thrive on the pressure and raise their performance level. In keeping with previous research on participants attempting to climb the world's highest mountain (e.g., Egan & Stelmack, 2003), Fletcher (2007) identified three key attributes that would be crucial in meeting the demands presented by the environment: self-belief, motivation, and focus. A high priority of the training programme was to develop confidence that remained as robust under pressure. Self-belief was also a critical factor at higher altitudes, where the most simple of tasks, such as putting on boots in the morning, can leave the fittest mountaineer breathless. Short-term goal setting was used, and visualization of the more complex climbing techniques became a particularly salient mental skill higher up the mountain.

With regard to motivation, Fletcher (2007) encouraged the trekkers and climbers to reflect on their motives and consider the fundamental reasons for their ambitions. He suggested this is a critical process, since only a small proportion of individuals who attempt to climb Mount Everest actually reach the summit successfully. He emphasized that developing mental toughness is not about creating ruthless and uncaring climbers with nerves of steel. Rather, his programme was designed to develop mentally tough performers who were highly motivated through their self-awareness, internal drive, and knowledge of when to re-group and return another day. Regarding focus, Fletcher's training programme emphasized that when under pressure, it is critical to maintain focus on "controllables" rather than "non-controllables", on the present, and on processes, positives, and composure. This focus strategy has also been found to be successful in previous mental toughness development programmes (see Goldberg, 1998; Sheard & Golby, 2006a). Thus, challenging environments would appear conducive to the development of mental toughness.

Cross-cultural/national differences

Most people hold beliefs about personality characteristics typical of members of their own and others' cultures (Peabody, 1985). These perceptions of national character may be generalizations from personal experience, stereotypes with a kernel of truth, or inaccurate stereotypes (Lee, Jussim, & McCauley, 1995; Macrae,

Stangor, & Hewstone, 1996). Stereotypes are oversimplified judgements. However, if they have some veracity, national character should reflect the average emotional, interpersonal, experiential, attitudinal, and motivational styles of members of the culture. Terracciano and co-workers concluded that their study of personality traits "offers the best evidence to date that in-group perceptions of national character may be informative about the culture, but they are not descriptive of the people themselves" (Terracciano et al., 2005, p. 99).

Little is known about the validity of relationships between mental toughness and the effects of culture. This is somewhat surprising since personalities may be shaped by one's cultural niche (Hofstede, 1984). Moving from cross-sectional studies of personality in sport within one country to cross-national studies represents a new and interesting direction in mental toughness research. Examining the effects of contextual variables on culture, and culture's effects on individuals and their personalities, is an accepted framework within cross-cultural studies (Segall, Dasen, Berry, & Poortinga, 1999). Further, it has been suggested that culture may be expressed in terms of culture values, or principles endorsed in a culture (Schwartz, 1994), which subsequently help shape the extent to which people will develop certain personality styles. Given this suggestion, therefore, it would be expected that the magnitude of the relationships between personality and successful sport performance would differ because of cultural influence (Glazer, Stetz, & Izso, 2004).

To date, cultural differences in coping strategies have been reported between Australian and US (Anshel, Williams, & Hodge, 1997), and Australian and Indonesian (Hoedaya & Anshel, 2003), competitive athletes. Differences have been found also in psychological characteristics between lacrosse players from five English-speaking countries (Heishman & Bunker, 1989), US and Chinese collegiate-level athletes (Cox & Liu, 1993), and US and British university soccer players (Mahoney & Todd, 1999). In particular, Heishman and Bunker reported on the significantly superior psychological attributes of the World Champion Australian lacrosse players. Interestingly, Golby et al. (2003) later reported that World Cup rugby league players who had learnt to play the game and were playing club rugby league in Australia at the time of the study had the highest level of mental toughness, while Sheard (in press) found that the Australian Universities rugby league team had significantly higher levels of mental toughness in comparison to their Great Britain opponents.

Australia enjoys success, and even dominance, in a variety of international sports, including cricket, cycling, hockey, rugby union, rugby league, and swimming (Anthony, 2007; Bierley, 2004). A fact similarly recognized by England rugby union international Josh Lewsey: "They [the Australians] have overachieved for generations. If you look at cricket, rugby union, swimming, tennis or rugby league, they have been outstanding" (Lewsey, 2007, p. 18). The Australian cricket Test (ranked 1) and One-Day (1987, 1999, 2003, 2007 World Champions) teams are the best in the world, appearing to possess "mental reserves like no other" (Nicholas, 2008, p. S24). That Australian national cricket teams have held the upper hand for two decades reveals a different psychology, of dramatically heightened mental toughness. It has been suggested of this pervasive culture of toughness, passed down through generations of cricketers, that mental toughness is *caught* via environmental influences (socialized) and *taught* through training (coached) (S. Gordon, Gucciardi, & Chambers, 2007). In other words, mental toughness is learned and can be developed. Writing of the necessity of developing heightened mental toughness to survive, let alone thrive, in international cricket, the fearsome former Australian fast bowler Dennis Lillee sums it up succinctly: "What you learn is that there are weak people and there are tough, strong people . . . there are two games going on out there, a mind game as well as a physical game of cricket, and you must never let anyone dominate you. The tough survive and the weak do not" (Lillee, 2003, p. 30).

The Australian rugby league team, The Kangaroos, is also the world's best (six consecutive World Cup titles between 1975 and 2000). It has been written of their domination that "belief is a powerful elixir and Australia's rugby league players have it by the bucket-load" (Irvine, 2003, p. 35). The Australian rugby union team, The Wallabies, have appeared in three World Cup Finals. They were World Champions in 1991 and 1999, and in losing the

2003 final, it was commented "any side but Australia would have capitulated . . . but Australia expect to beat England" (Barnes, 2003, p. 38). They consistently stand proud atop the Commonwealth Games medals table. Even in a sport considered "minority" in Australia, its soccer team, The Socceroos, was unlucky to lose to the eventual tournament winners, Italy, in the 2006 FIFA World Cup.

The Australian mentally tough mindset has, on many occasions, been a psychological hurdle for, in particular, their English/British sporting counterparts. Examples are numerous in cricket, hockey, rugby league, and rugby union. In the face of seemingly psychologically superior opposition, unsurprisingly, English/British sporting failures have been attributed to the lack of a mentally tough mindset. It has been suggested that "English and British sport in the past few decades has been one long tale of disappointments, nearlys, what ifs, buts, apologies, explanations and excuses, which together form a deepening psychological accommodation with failure" (Anthony, 2007, p. 41). In addition, there exists a cultural acceptance of worshipping sport performers, who, ultimately, have failed (Reed, 2007). Similar observations have been made in New Zealand, where yet another Rugby World Cup failure manifested for the pre-tournament favourite All Blacks (Drake, 2007; Loe, 2007).

The German national soccer team is a product with a proven track record. Germany has won the World Cup three times, has been runners-up on four occasions, and has been involved in the decisive match in six out of the last ten European Championship Finals, winning three of them. Brazil (5) and Italy (4) aside in terms of the number of World Cup triumphs, no other country can match this record. The reason behind this success? The suggestion put forward by Franz Beckenbauer, and he should know as the only man to have lifted the World Cup on separate occasions as player (1974) and coach (1990), is extremely convincing: "The German mentality is stronger than that of other nations. I can assure you Germany does not have better players, but even when they are under pressure they seem to maintain a winning mentality" (as cited in Cameron, 1995, p. 109). This "mentality" is summed up wonderfully, when, interviewed during the 2008 European

Championship, Czech Republic goalkeeper Petr Čech spoke of the mental strength of his German counterpart, Jens Lehmann: "there are doubts about his level of performances after spending most of the season on the bench. That should not influence him and that is his biggest strength – mentally he is very powerful and nothing seems to faze him" (as cited in Balague, 2008, p. 15).

Similarly, of his three highly favourable years at Bayern Munich, Germany's most famous and successful club, Scottish international footballer Allan McInally recalled: "You knew your place and refined your aims and ambitions accordingly. The rules bring a sort of determination with them. The practice games were never 10–8 but more like 2–1. Training was never a laugh. It was your job and you did it right" (as cited in Cameron, 1995, p. 112). And this was rewarded. "The players came first . . . The players are always looked after. They receive the most respect," McInally added (as cited in Cameron, p. 111). The environment that surrounds Bayern Munich and, in particular, the German national team is conducive to achievement. The recognition and trappings of success come with responsibility.

An interesting comparison can be drawn with Denmark. Surveys over 30 years have shown that the Danes score higher than any other Western country on measures of life satisfaction (Layard, 2006; Turner, 2007). There is a valuable lesson to be learned from the Danes' celebration of ordinariness: an ease and contentment with oneself, a quiet competence, and a confidence borne out of exclusivity. This is summed up in the Danish word *tilfreds*, meaning, literally, "at peace". Parallels can be drawn between an appropriate mindset for sport and contentment. Contentment is having a comfortable lifestyle without being swept up by competitive consumption. It is a feeling of belonging, of knowing and accepting the rules of the club. The development of mental toughness involves athletes and coaches realizing that sport is to be enjoyed and that winning is not the sole purpose of sport (Barnes, 2008c). An all-consuming ambition with coming out top is unhealthy and does not develop mental toughness. Moreover, such ambition in the absence of mental toughness is wholly unrealistic. Indeed, wanting to win more than anyone else can become obsessive and the inevitable letdown, when it happens, is palpable.

Rather, the obsession should not be with winning, but with putting everything in place that increases the likelihood of victory, in particular, the development of athletes' mental toughness; for example, supportive home environments; motivational, rewarding, and enjoyable training environments; challenging experiences; exposure to realistic competition; and PST programmes each have a vital role.

Athletes ought to have *tilfreds*: an inner peace and calm that comes from doing all one can to secure victory. Possession of an inner calm and mental toughness are perfectly compatible bedfellows, operating harmoniously to result in higher subjective well-being. As American Olympic great Michael Johnson reflected of one particular group's underperformance in the 2008 Beijing Olympics: "British athletes must train harder and smarter . . . and develop a tougher attitude to compete with the American, Caribbean and African athletes who generally approach competition with a tougher attitude and approach" (Johnson, 2008, p. V5). Commitment to mental toughness development from the aforementioned sources would address the concern that "we want to win. We want to win as much if not more than anyone else. We just do not want to do what is necessary to win" (Anthony, 2007, p. 41).

Conclusion

Not only is it crucial for athletes to develop their mental toughness in order to increase the likelihood of their reaching the highest competitive standards, but they must also identify what it takes to stay there. Researchers have stated "there should be equal concern over what it takes to retain that expertise" (Starkes, Weir, Singh, Hodges, & Kerr, 1999, p. 284). Indeed, it is often considered that to be a true champion, one must be able to retain excellence (Abbott & Collins, 2004). The development and maintenance of a mentally tough mindset will facilitate the necessary adjustments.

On their way to the sporting summit, athletes will encounter confrontations, setbacks, mistakes, and unavoidable failures, along with successes and satisfactions. Obstacles are an inevitable part of the developmental process. Sustained success comes from training and performing well over the long term rather than winning in the short term (Balyi & Hamilton, 2004). Just as there is no shortcut to success in athletic preparation, so the development of mental toughness is a long-term process. In particular, understanding of this will facilitate successful PST programme outcomes.

The more we invest in something, the more commitment we feel toward it. This is not to confuse investment with expenditure. Investment implies a return of significant personal value from a particular outlay. Surely more athletes would invest in appropriate PST if, in return, they develop into psychologically complete athletes with highly developed levels of mental toughness. Such performers would possess a competitive mind; be assertive, forceful, dominant; display commitment, eagerness, passion; have a high level of game intelligence; be focused, tremendously disciplined; and supremely self-confident.

In a recent newspaper interview, former England international cricketer Graeme Hick reflected on whether he ought to have been mentally tougher during his test career: "At school in Zim [Zimbabwe] I was taught to play sport to your best, to respect opponents and play it in the right spirit. Only when I played here [England] did it start to get an 'edge' and that's got more intense in the last few years" (as cited in S. Hughes, 2008, p. S13). It is illuminating that the player he most admires is former Australian captain Steve Waugh who was, arguably, the poster boy for mental toughness in cricket. Noted for his game intelligence, in particular his perception, reasoning, and decision-making, Waugh was a consummate tactician who visualized options, responded to changes in the pattern of play, and modified his team to suit environmental conditions. He was much admired by many of his contemporaries, including Hick, who spoke of Waugh's mental toughness: "his patience and discipline were amazing. He was one of the hardest characters in the game" (as cited in S. Hughes, p. S13). Clearly, Steve Waugh's mental toughness elevated fellow cricketers' respect for him. Fittingly, and with typical insightfulness, the former Australian captain's shall be the final words on the benefits of developing a mentally tough mindset: "Having a reputation for being mentally tough can have enormous advantages, because opponents respect and admire that trait and will put you on a pedestal, while teammates also hold you in higher esteem" (Waugh, 2006, p. 645).

6   Concluding mental toughness

Keep away from people who try to belittle your ambitions. Small
people always do that, but the really great make you feel that you,
too, can become great.

Mark Twain

Concluding commentary

As we approach the end of a considerable journey, we now know
what is constitutive of mental toughness, how it has been conceptualized, that it can be measured with reliable and valid instruments, and, crucially, how it can be developed and maintained.
Mental toughness is an attribute that can be learned. The complex
nature of mental toughness has been discussed throughout the
book. To conclude, I would like to proffer the possibility that an
element of mental toughness may be genetic. Indeed, such a
suggestion has been advanced previously by international sport
performers: "Mental toughness is having the natural or developed
psychological edge that enables you to . . ." (G. Jones et al., 2002,
p. 209). By "natural", these athletes were suggesting that such an
attribute might be innate as well as developed over many years of
experience. I hasten to emphasize the "as well as", and the absence
of "rather than".

Perspectives on explaining successful sport performance vary,
considering factors such as hereditary contributors (Bouchard &
Malina, 1984; Bouchard, Malina, & Pérusse, 1997) and the role of
dedicated practice over many years (Ericsson & Charness, 1994;

Ericsson, Krampe, & Tesch-Römer, 1993). Because the attainment of the highest levels of performance in sport depends on so many variables, it is not easy to partial out the role of heredity. The premise that genetic determinants are as powerful as experiences and environments in life is not new. However, though recent research has begun to claim links between genes and performance (Pérusse, Rankinen, Rauramaa, Rivera, Wolfarth, & Bouchard, 2003), little has been discussed in relation to how this information might be used to modify specific sporting performance.

It is commonly believed that highly successful performers are talented individuals. Their success is often attributed to complex, domain-specific cognitive structures and skills that are acquired as a consequence of attaining a sequence of increasingly challenging goals over extended periods of time (Ericsson, 1996; Ericsson & Charness, 1994; Ericsson et al., 1993). On the basis of such research, Ericsson and Lehmann (1996), and later Ericsson (2003), argued that expert performance is attributable to prolonged periods of deliberate practice, rather than the presence of any innate talent.

An alternative view is that athletic talent is based, at least in some part, on a genetic predisposition that is responsive to training intervention. There is evidence to suggest that these theoretical positions are not mutually exclusive, and that both environmental and genetic factors interact in contributing to successful sport performance. No one with any understanding of genetics believes that genes entirely explain behavioural traits, accepting as Matt Ridley put it that nature works via nurture (Ridley, 2003).

Personality characteristics are moderately heritable (Rushton, Bons, & Hur, 2008; Zuckerman, 2005), and we know that certain genetic combinations leave people more susceptible to environmental triggers. Yet, little is known about the potential inheritance of mental toughness or mental toughness as phenotype. Using the MT48 questionnaire, mental toughness subscale heritability estimates of between .36 and .56 were reported in a sample of 219 pairs of adult twins (Horsburgh, Schermer, Veselka, & Vernon, 2009). The authors reported that 52 per cent of the variation in total mental toughness was due to genetic factors. Interestingly, given the differences observed in MT48 subscale heritability estimates and that those attributes influenced by environmental triggers may be more malleable than those influenced by genetic factors (Cloninger, 2000; Cloninger, Svrakic, & Przybeck, 1993), Horsburgh et al. suggested that it may be easier to develop specific mental toughness attributes rather than mental toughness as a whole.

In sport, researchers have just begun to explore the relationship between genetic make-up and personality. For example, the relationship between the specific genotype of the serotonin transporter 5-hydroxytryptamine (5-HTT) gene, which is proposed to moderate reactions to stress, and positive psychological characteristics in young swimmers has been examined (Golby & Sheard, 2006). While no significant associations were observed, possibly as a result of the small sample size and that the participants had not yet specialized in a single competitive distance, the relationship between genotype and psychological characteristics in sport performers remains a particularly intriguing area for further research.

I am not for one moment suggesting that there are direct causal relationships between genes and, for example, mental toughness. Specifically, genetic influences do not imply that personality is both biological and unchangeable (Caspi, Roberts, & Shiner, 2005; Kagan, 1999; Plomin, DeFries, McClearn, & McGuffin, 2001). Nobody inherits an unalterable capacity for mental toughness. What would be the point of PST programmes if people's levels of mental toughness, or even constituent parts, were genetically predetermined? Environment is crucial. The brain is "plastic", adapting and sharpening according to the experiences it has (LeDoux, 2002). More probable is that the quality of exceptional sport performers arises from a unique combination of inherited traits and capacities developed through training, experience, and exposure to challenging, yet supportive, environments; that is, an interaction. I believe this interaction is summarized succinctly by Lance Armstrong: "It takes a lot of hard work, a lot of natural talent" (Armstrong, 2008, p. 2); environment being the former, and heredity accounting for the latter. However, any genetic component of mental toughness is, for now, speculation. Much more research needs to be conducted in this area before the null hypothesis can be rejected.

Other directions for future mental toughness research

Future studies may also consider investigating how mental toughness relates to other constructs contributing to the positive psychology movement (e.g., flow, happiness, hope). Other constructs,
for example passion (Vallerand et al., 2003), whose recent exploration relative to the sport domain has yielded promising findings
(e.g., Amiot, Vallerand, & Blanchard, 2006; Sheard & Golby, 2009;
Vallerand & Miquelon, 2007), offer opportunities to assess further
the construct validation of mental toughness. Longitudinal studies
would afford the possibility of, for example, examining further the
effects of PST interventions and outdoor adventure education
activities on levels of mental toughness, related positive psychological attributes, and performance. Research should also consider
the moderating role of mental toughness in the development of
high-quality interpersonal relationships (e.g., coach–athlete,
parent–athlete).

In addition, given the increasing prevalence and severity of
injury in, for example, high-impact collision sports such as rugby
league (Gabbett, 2000; Meir, McDonald, & Russell, 1997; D. M.
O'Connor, 2004), and rugby union (Cleary, 2005a; Gallagher,
2005; Slot, 2005), longitudinal research would allow the recording
and monitoring of athletes' mental toughness and positive psychological profile during the rehabilitation process. Given the ever-
increasing media scrutiny and game-related pressures facing sport
referees and umpires, consideration should be given to how mental
toughness manifests in sport officiating. A recent study found that
professional rugby league referees were as mentally tough as the
players they were officiating (Sheard & Golby, 2008). This research
needs to be extended across a variety of sports. How mental
toughness relates to athletes' sportsmanship (and gamesmanship)
behaviours should also be addressed.

The worldwide nurturing of positive psychology, and mental
toughness specifically, offers great potential for cross-cultural
research. As mentioned in Chapter 4, work has begun on the
translation of the PPI-A and the SMTQ into other languages. This
will enable their utilization by non-English speaking sport performers. Establishing each of the scales' psychometric properties in

other languages will afford the opportunity to examine further how mental toughness may be influenced by cultural factors.

Conclusion

Mental toughness has been criticized for being a potentially revealing measure that has devolved, rather than evolved, and for its being a misused and abused term "thrown about with impunity" (Carlstadt, 2004, p. 225). This book has been a response to such observations, and has shown mental toughness to be a potent construct with instruments sufficiently sensitive to measure psychological performance. Indeed, the psychometrically robust PPI-A and SMTQ inventories presented in Chapter 4 refute the assertion that "a personality inventory does not exist to measure the trait of mental toughness independent of other personality traits" (Cox, 2007, p. 31).

Sporting events are often won or lost between the ears. Mental toughness elevates those athletes who have it above the rest. A hardened, disciplined mindset differentiates between the good and the great, especially at the highest levels of competition. Being mentally tough reflects positive values: responsibility, self-belief, and positivity to challenge. Mentally tough athletes have confidence and a winning mentality. They have strength of character and are able to bounce back from mistakes. They are steadfast, persistent, and have a conviction about their purpose. They live in the moment and deal with what is in front of them, recognizing that the future will arrive in its own good time.

Mental toughness is the "edge", the "X factor", if you like. I prefer the "A factor": "A" for achievement. A high level of mental toughness gives individuals and teams an overwhelming advantage. If physical and technical skills are matched, and environmental conditions do not favour inequitably an individual or team, it is those who are mentally stronger that prevail. In training and competition situations that are pivotal to success, athletes with heightened mental toughness are able to perform to their best when it counts the most. Mentally tough athletes are able to combine striving for personal excellence with competitive success. At the same time, they are also able to encourage fairness and respect for the rules/laws of their sport and opponents. These are the exceptional individuals, the leaders who rise to the moment, the champions who possess the virtues to excel, the victors who win with integrity – the "Achievers".

Successful sport performance is, ultimately, about talent and mental toughness. Without denying the crucial role of talent, though which by itself is insufficient, I have tried to present a case that it is something else that distinguishes the greatest athletes – an achievement mindset. The determination, commitment, self-belief, positive cognition, emotional discipline, and perseverance necessary for success are each constitutive of the achievement mindset that I call mental toughness. I would go further; arguably, it is mental toughness that makes someone a supremely talented sport performer.

References

Abbott, A., & Collins, D. (2004). Eliminating the dichotomy between theory and practice in talent identification and development: Considering the role of psychology. *Journal of Sports Sciences, 22,* 395–408.

Abi-Hashem, N. (2001). Rediscovering hope in American psychology. *American Psychologist, 56,* 85–86.

Aidman, E., & Schofield, G. (2004). Personality and individual differences in sport. In T. Morris & J. Summers (Eds.), *Sport psychology: Theory, applications and issues* (2nd ed., pp. 22–47). Milton, Australia: Wiley.

Alderman, R. B. (1974). *Psychological behavior in sport.* Toronto, Canada: W.B. Saunders Company.

Allen, J. (2007). *Michael Schumacher: The edge of greatness.* London: Headline.

Allen, T. W. (1988). The cognitive bases of peak performance: A classroom intervention with student athletes. *Journal of Counseling and Development, 67,* 202–204.

Amiot, C. E., Vallerand, R. J., & Blanchard, C. M. (2006). Passion and psychological adjustment: A test of the person-environment fit hypothesis. *Personality and Social Psychology Bulletin, 32,* 220–229.

Andrew, M., Grobbelaar, H. W., & Potgieter, J. C. (2007). Sport psychological skill levels and related psycho-social factors that distinguish between rugby union players of different participation levels. *South African Journal for Research in Sport, Physical Education and Recreation, 29,* 1–15.

Anshel, M. H. (2001). Qualitative validation of a model for coping with acute stress in sport. *Journal of Sport Behavior, 24,* 223–246.

Anshel, M. H., Williams, L. R. T., & Hodge, K. (1997). Cross-cultural and gender differences on coping style in sport. *International Journal of Sport Psychology, 28,* 141–156.

Anthony, A. (2007, November 25). Born to lose. *Observer Sports Monthly*, pp. 36–46.

Armstrong, L. (2008). To raise cancer awareness, the cyclist is returning to the road. *Time*, Vol. *172*(16), p. 2 (10 Questions).

Atella, M. D. (1999). Case studies in the development of organizational hardiness: From theory to practice. *Consulting Psychology Journal: Practice and Research*, *51*, 125–134.

Atherton, M. (2003, July 21). Two souls laid bare in the ultimate of tests. *The Times*, pp. 20–21 (The Game).

Atherton, M. (2008, September 29). Shah should be beneficiary from Vaughan's absence for India tour. *The Times*, p. 68 (Sport).

Atherton, M. (2009, February 12). Stand by Bell? It's an open-and-shut case. *The Times*, p. 75 (Sport).

Baker, A. (2008, July 5). Laura Robson proves she is real deal. *The Daily Telegraph*, p. S5 (Sport).

Balague, G. (2008, June 9). Buffon is best of breed but Casillas could be top dog. *The Times*, p. 15 (The Game).

Balyi, I., & Hamilton, A. (2003, Issue 20). Long-term athlete development update: Trainability in childhood and adolescence. *Faster Higher Stronger*, pp. 6–8.

Balyi, I., & Hamilton, A. (2004, Spring). Long term athlete development: Trainability in childhood and adolescence. *Olympic Coach*, pp. 4–8.

Bandura, A. (1997). *Self-efficacy: The exercise of control*. New York: Freeman.

Barlow, C. (2006, December 22). Fletcher and his team's mindset was all wrong [Letter to the editor]. *The Daily Telegraph*, p. S17 (Sport).

Barnard, C. P. (1994). Resilience: A shift in our perception? *American Journal of Family Therapy*, *22*, 135–144.

Barnes, S. (2003, November 24). Where our rugby boys have led, the rest can follow. *The Times*, p. 38 (Sport).

Barnes, S. (2005, May 26). The miracle of Istanbul. *The Times*, p. 96 (Sport).

Barnes, S. (2008a, January 7). Let he who has never sledged complain about others sledging. *The Times*, p. 61 (Sport).

Barnes, S. (2008b, January 8). Sledging was always going to put the game on slippery slope. *The Times*, p. 65 (Sport).

Barnes, S. (2008c, January 11). The ten commandments to remind us that sport was always meant to be fun. *The Times*, p. 94 (Sport).

Barnes, S. (2008d, January 14). Winning is not everything. *The Times*, p. 66 (Sport).

Barnes, S. (2008e, January 21). Federer shows qualities that go into making true champion. *The Times*, p. 71 (Sport).

Barnes, S. (2008f, March 24). How swearing became a national sport. *The Times*, p. 23.

Barnes, S. (2009, February 23). Cautious Strauss helps rebirth of a cricketing force. *The Times*, p. 63 (Sport).

Bartone, P. T. (1999). Hardiness protects against war-related stress in army reserve forces. *Consulting Psychology Journal, 51*, 72–83.

Basic Behavioral Science Task Force of the National Advisory Mental Health Council. (1996). Basic behavioral science research for mental health: Vulnerability and resilience. *American Psychologist, 51*, 22–28.

Berkow, I. (2006, September 30). Fragile quarterback shows some mental toughness. *The New York Times*. Retrieved October 2, 2006, from http://www.nytimes.com.

Bianco, T. (2001). Social support and recovery from sport injury: Elite skiers share their experiences. *Research Quarterly for Exercise and Sport, 72*, 376–388.

Bierley, S. (2004, August 24). Awesome Aussies continue to exert their sporting dominance. *The Guardian*, pp. 6–7 (Sport).

Bierley, S. (2009, March 23). Nadal replaces Federer as the standard setter for Murray. *The Guardian*. Retrieved March 23, 2009, from http://www.guardian.co.uk/sport.

Bloom, B. S. (Ed.). (1985). *Developing talent in young people.* New York: Ballantine.

Bolton, P. (2008, May 12). Jones to start Sale inquest. *The Daily Telegraph*, p. S27 (Sport).

Bonanno, G. (2004). Loss, trauma, and human resilience: Have we underestimated the human capacity to thrive after extremely aversive events? *American Psychologist, 51*, 72–82.

Booth, L. (2008, October 7). England opt for army boot camp in readiness for Stanford. *The Guardian*, p. 8 (Sport).

Bouchard, C., & Malina, R. M. (1984). Genetics and Olympic athletes: A discussion of methods and issues. In J. E. L. Carter (Ed.), *Kinanthropology of Olympic athletes* (pp. 28–38). Basel, Switzerland: Karger.

Bouchard, C., Malina, R. M., & Pérusse, L. (1997). *Genetics of fitness and physical performance.* Champaign, IL: Human Kinetics.

Boycott, G. (2005, September 13). Warne lets the urn slip from his grasp. *The Daily Telegraph*, p. S6 (Sport).

Boycott, G. (2009, February 23). I fear Flintoff Test days numbered. *The Daily Telegraph*, p. S21 (Sport).

Braddock, J. H., Royster, D. A., Winfield, L. F., & Hawkins, R. (1991). Bouncing back: Sports and academic resilience among African-American males. *Education and Urban Society, 24*, 113–131.

Brewer, J., & Davis, J. (1995). Applied physiology of rugby league. *Sports Medicine, 13,* 129–135.

Bronson, J., Gibson, S., Kichar, R., & Priest, S. (1992). Evaluation of team development in a corporate adventure training program. *Journal of Experiential Education, 15,* 50–53.

Brookes, A. (2003). A critique of neo-Hahnian outdoor education theory. Part one: Challenges to the concept of "character building". *Journal of Adventure Education and Outdoor Learning, 3,* 49–62.

Brown, O. (2007, December 3). Villa and United renew rivalry. *The Daily Telegraph,* p. S1 (Sport).

Brown, O. (2008a, October 6). Brown's stock on the rise. *The Daily Telegraph,* p. S2 (Sport).

Brown, O. (2008b, November 3). Benitez stunned at reversal. *The Daily Telegraph,* p. S13 (Sport).

Bull, S. J., Albinson, J. G., & Shambrook, C. J. (1996). *The mental game plan: Getting psyched for sport.* Eastbourne, England: Sports Dynamics.

Bull, S. J., Shambrook, C. J., James, W., & Brooks, J. E. (2005). Towards an understanding of mental toughness in elite English cricketers. *Journal of Applied Sport Psychology, 17,* 209–227.

Byers, T. (2004). Managing sport operations, quality and performance. In J. Beech & S. Chadwick (Eds.), *The business of sport management* (pp. 240–267). London: Pearson.

Cadigan, N. (2008, April 18). Jack Gibson: Played strong, done good. *The Daily Telegraph* (Australia). Retrieved August 30, 2008, from http://www.dailytelegraph.com.au/sport.

Cain, N. (2008, March 30). Where there's life, there's hope for Leeds. *The Times,* p. 16 (Sport).

Cameron, C. (1995). *Football, Fussball, Voetbal: The European Game 1955 – Euro96.* London: BBC Books.

Carboni, J., Burke, K. L., Joyner, A. B., Hardy, C. J., & Blom, L. C. (2002). The effects of brief imagery on free throw shooting performance and concentrational style of intercollegiate basketball players: A single-subject design. *International Sports Journal, 6,* 60–67.

Carlstadt, R. A. (2004). *Critical moments during competition: A mind-body model of sport performance when it counts the most.* New York: Psychology Press.

Cash, P. (2008, June 22). Federer's case for the defence. *The Sunday Times,* pp. 6–7 (Sport).

Cashmore, E. (2002). *Sport psychology: The key concepts.* London: Routledge.

Cashmore, E. (2005). *Making sense of sports* (4th ed.). London: Routledge.

Cason, D., & Gillis, H. L. (1994). A meta-analysis of outdoor adventure programming with adolescents. *Journal of Experiential Education, 17,* 40–47.

Caspi, A., Roberts, B. W., & Shiner, R. L. (2005). Personality development: Stability and change. *Annual Review of Psychology, 56,* 453–484.

Cattell, R. B. (1957). *Personality and motivation structure and measurement.* New York: Harcourt, Brace, and World.

Cattell, R. B., Blewett, D. B., & Beloff, J. R. (1955). The inheritance of personality. A multiple variance analysis determination of approximate nature-nurture ratios for primary personality factors in Q-data. *American Journal of Human Genetics, 7,* 122–146.

Celebi, M., & Ozen, G. (2004, March). University students and adventure education programmes: A study of meanings and experience of adventure training activities. In W. Krause (Chair), *Outdoor and adventure education – developments and programmes.* Symposium conducted at the meeting of the International Conference on Leisure, Tourism & Sport – Education, Integration, Innovation, Cologne, Germany.

Chadband, I. (2009, February 21). Return of the messiah. *The Daily Telegraph,* p. S24 (Sport).

Chamorro-Premuzic, T., & Furnham, A. (2006). Self-assessed intelligence and academic performance. *Educational Psychology, 26,* 769–779.

Cleary, M. (2005a, January 11). Injury crisis is sending game to intensive care. *The Daily Telegraph,* p. S6 (Sport).

Cleary, M. (2005b, February 8). Tales of the unexpected are talk of the town. *The Daily Telegraph,* p. S6 (Sport).

Cleary, M. (2007, October 15). England heroes defy odds and logic for one final fling. *The Daily Telegraph,* pp. S2–S3 (Sport).

Cleary, M. (2008, September 5). World's top players can raise bar again in Guinness Premiership. *The Daily Telegraph,* p. S12 (Sport).

Cleary, M. (2009a, February 13). Shaun Edwards is a man close to Wales' heart. *The Daily Telegraph.* Retrieved February 13, 2009, from http://www.dailytelegraph.co.uk/sport.

Cleary, M. (2009b, February 23). Gritty Wasps steal contentious win. *The Daily Telegraph,* pp. S14–S15.

Cloninger, C. R. (2000). Biology of personality dimensions. *Current Opinions in Psychiatry, 13,* 611–616.

Cloninger, C. R., Svrakic, D. M., & Przybeck, T. R. (1993). A psychobiological model of temperament and character. *Archives of General Psychiatry, 50,* 975–990.

Clough, P., Earle, K., & Sewell, D. (2002). Mental toughness: The concept and its measurement. In I. Cockerill (Ed.), *Solutions in sport psychology* (pp. 32–45). London: Thomson.

Coe, S. (2004, August 30). Mental strength the key to an Olympic double to savour. *The Daily Telegraph*, p. S3 (Sport).

Cohn, P. J. (1990). An exploratory study on sources of stress and athlete burnout in youth golf. *The Sport Psychologist, 4*, 95–106.

Cohn, P. J. (1991). An exploratory study on peak performance in golf. *The Sport Psychologist, 5*, 1–14.

Comrey, A. L. (1994). *Revised manual and handbook for the Comrey Personality Scales.* San Diego, CA: Educational and Industrial Testing Services.

Comrey, A. L., & Lee, H. B. (1992). *A first course in factor analysis* (2nd ed.). Mahwah, NJ: Erlbaum.

Connaughton, D., Wadey, R., Hanton, S., & Jones, G. (2008). The development and maintenance of mental toughness. *Journal of Sports Sciences, 26*, 83–95.

Conquering Heroes. (2003, November 24). *The Guardian*, p. 21.

Conroy, D. E. (2001). Fear of failure: An exemplar for social development research in sport. *Quest, 53*, 165–183.

Corry, M. (2007, October 15). Now we're the rugby version of Jamaica's bobsleigh team. *The Guardian*, p. 3 (Sport).

Côté, J. (2001). Coach and peer influence on children's development through sport. In J. M. Silva & D. E. Stevens (Eds.), *Psychological foundations of sport* (pp. 520–540). Boston, MA: Allyn & Bacon.

Côté, J., Salmela, J. H., Trudel, P., Baria, A., & Russell, S. J. (1995). The coaching model: A grounded assessment of expertise gymnastic coaches' knowledge. *Journal of Sport and Exercise Psychology, 17*, 1–17.

Coward, M. (2006, November, 27). Mental toughness is essential. *The Australian.* Retrieved August 30, 2008, from http://www.theaustralian.com.au/sport.

Cox, R. H. (2007). *Sport psychology: Concepts and applications* (6th ed.). New York: McGraw-Hill.

Cox, R. H., & Liu, Z. (1993). Psychological skills: A cross-cultural investigation. *Journal of Sport and Exercise Psychology, 16*, 135–149.

Crossman, J. (1997). Psychological rehabilitation from sports injuries. *Sports Medicine, 23*, 333–339.

Crust, L., & Clough, P. J. (2005). Relationship between mental toughness and physical endurance, *Perceptual and Motor Skills, 100*, 192–194.

Cumming, S. P., Smoll, F. L., Smith, R. E., & Grossbard, J. R. (2007). Is winning everything? The relative contributions of motivational climate and won-lost percentage in youth sports. *Journal of Applied Sport Psychology*, *19*, 322–336.

Curtis Management Group. (1998). *Motivation Lombardi style*. Lombard, IL: Celebrating Excellence Publishing.

Dall, J. (2007, December 19). Wenger proud of passion. *Sky Sports News*. Retrieved December 19, 2007, from http://www.skysports.com.

Dallaglio, L. (2007). *In the blood*. London: Headline.

Danish, S. J., Petitpas, A. J., & Hale, B. D. (1993). Life development intervention for athletes: Life skills through sports. *The Counseling Psychologist*, *21*, 352–385.

Davies, G. (2003, November 24). Europe can benefit from shift in balance of power. *The Times*, p. 36 (Sport).

Davies, G. (2007, October 19). While there is more than one way to play the game, there is only one objective for the defending champions tomorrow after their return to core values. *The Times*, p. 19 (The Final).

Davies, J. (2008, June 15). Decisions made the difference. *The Independent on Sunday*, p. 86 (Sport).

Deaner, H., & Silva, J. M. (2001). Personality and sport performance. In J. M. Silva & D. E. Stevens (Eds.), *Psychological foundations of sport* (pp. 48–65). Boston, MA: Allyn & Bacon.

Dennis, P. W. (1981). Mental toughness and the athlete. *Ontario Physical and Health Education Association*, *7*, 37–40.

Dickinson, M. (2009, February 23). Special event. *The Times*, p. 9 (The Game).

Dixon, P. (2009, April 6). Guru's gadgetry helps Padraig Harrington prepare for Augusta. *The Times*. Retrieved April 6, 2009, from http://www.timesonline.co.uk/tol/sport.

Dongsung, S. S., & Kang-Heon, L. (1994). A comparative study of mental toughness between elite and non-elite female athletes. *Korean Journal of Sport Science*, *6*, 85–102.

Dorfman, H. A. (2003). *Coaching the mental game*. Lanham, MD: Taylor Trade.

Drake, J. (2007, October 8). Pressure cooker once again proves too hot for All Blacks. *New Zealand Herald*. Retrieved December 15, 2007, from http://www.nzherald.co.nz.

Driediger, M., Hall, C., & Callow, N. (2006). Imagery use by injured athletes: A qualitative analysis. *Journal of Sports Sciences*, *24*, 261–271.

Durand-Bush, N., & Salmela, J. H. (2002). The development and maintenance of expert athletic performance: Perceptions of World and Olympic champions. *Journal of Applied Sport Psychology*, *14*, 154–171.

Dweck, C. (2006). *Mindset: The psychology of success.* Toronto, Canada: Random House.

Edwards, S. (2008, February 29). Cipriani too good to be sitting out games on England's bench. *The Guardian*, p. 9 (Sport).

Egan, S., & Stelmack, R. M. (2003). A personality profile of Mount Everest climbers. *Personality and Individual Differences, 34*, 1491–1494.

Eklund, R. C. (1994). A season long investigation of competitive cognition in collegiate wrestlers. *Research Quarterly for Exercise and Sport, 65*, 169–183.

Eklund, R. C. (1996). Preparing to compete: A season-long investigation with collegiate wrestlers. *The Sport Psychologist, 10*, 111–131.

Elliott, B. (2008, June 22). Tiger's genuine gesture makes him the all-time sporting great. *The Observer*, p. 9 (Sport).

Ellis, C. (2005, September 13). Pietersen walks tall as the nation celebrates. *The Daily Telegraph*, pp. IV–V (The Ashes 2005).

Emms, G. (2009, April 10). My chance to inspire self-confidence in the young. *The Times*. Retrieved April 10, 2009, from http://www.times online.co.uk/tol/sport.

Ericsson, K. A. (Ed.). (1996). *The road to excellence: The acquisition of expert performance in the arts and sciences, sports and games.* Mahwah, NJ: Erlbaum.

Ericsson, K. A. (2003). Development of elite performance and deliberate practice: An update from the perspective of the expert performance approach. In J. L. Starkes & K. A. Ericsson (Eds.), *Expert performance in sports: Advances in research on sport expertise* (pp. 49–83). Champaign, IL: Human Kinetics.

Ericsson, K. A., & Charness, N. (1994). Expert performance: Its structure and acquisition. *American Psychologist, 49*, 725–747.

Ericsson, K. A., Krampe, R. T., & Tesch-Römer, C. (1993). The role of deliberate practice in the acquisition of expert performance. *Psychological Review, 100*, 363–406.

Ericsson, K. A., & Lehmann, A. C. (1996). Expert and exceptional performance: Evidence on maximal adaptations on task constraints. *Annual Review of Psychology, 47*, 273–305.

Eysenck, H. J., Nias, D. K. B., & Cox, D. N. (1982). Sport and personality. *Advances in Behavior Research and Therapy, 4*, 1–56.

Faulkner, G. (2006, September 30). Who's a clever boy? *New Scientist*, p. 27 (Letter to the Editor).

Favret, B., & Benzel, D. (1997). *Complete guide to water skiing.* Champaign, IL: Human Kinetics.

Firfield, D. (2009, April 2). Hats off to Capello as steely England show new-found strength. *The Guardian*. Retrieved April 2, 2009, from http://www.guardian.co.uk/sport.

Fletcher, D. (2005). "Mental toughness" and human performance: Definitional, conceptual and theoretical issues. *Journal of Sports Sciences, 23*, 1246–1247.

Fletcher, D. (2007, December). Toughness training on the world's highest mountain. *The Sport and Exercise Scientist*, pp. 10–11.

Fletcher, D., & Fletcher, J. (2005). A meta-model of stress, emotions and performance: Conceptual foundations, theoretical framework, and research directions. *Journal of Sports Sciences, 23*, 157–158.

Fletcher, D. (2008, September 30). Vaughan still has qualities to do a job for England. *The Guardian*, p. 9 (Sport).

Fourie, S., & Potgieter, J. R. (2001). The nature of mental toughness in sport. *South African Journal for Research in Sport, Physical Education and Recreation, 23*, 63–72.

Frankl, V. E. (1959). *Man's search for meaning: An introduction to logotherapy*. Boston, MA: Beacon Press.

Fraser, A. (2004, October 12). Miller, "invincible" who defied Messerschmitts, dies in Melbourne at 84. *The Independent*, p. 58 (Sport).

Gabbett, T. J. (2000). Incidence, site, and nature of injuries in amateur rugby league over three consecutive seasons. *British Journal of Sports Medicine, 34*, 98–103.

Gallagher, B. (2005, June 27). Video footage supports emotional O'Driscoll. *The Daily Telegraph*, p. S1 (Sport).

Galli, N., & Vealey, R. S. (2008). "Bouncing back" from adversity: Athletes' experiences of resilience. *The Sport Psychologist, 22*, 316–335.

Garside, K. (2008, March 2). Fitter means faster. *The Sunday Times*, p. 15 (Sport).

Garza, D. L., & Feltz, D. L. (1998). Effects of selected mental practice techniques on performance ratings, self-efficacy, and state anxiety of competitive figure skaters. *The Sport Psychologist, 12*, 1–15.

Gaudreau, P., & Blondin, J-P. (2002). Development of a questionnaire for the assessment of coping strategies employed by athletes in competitive sport settings. *Psychology of Sport and Exercise, 3*, 1–34.

Gendlin, E. T. (1966). Existentialism and experiential psychotherapy. In C. Moustakas (Ed.), *The child's discovery of himself* (pp. 196–236). New York: Basic Books.

Giacobbi, P. R., Foore, B., & Weinberg, R. S. (2004). Broken clubs and expletives: The sources of stress and coping responses of skilled and moderately skilled golfers. *Journal of Applied Sport Psychology, 16*, 166–182.

Giacobbi, P. R., Lynn, T. K., Wetherington, J. M., Jenkins, J., Bodendorf, M., & Langley, B. (2004). Stress and coping during the transition to university for first-year female athletes. *The Sport Psychologist, 18*, 1–20.

Gibson, A. (1998). *Mental toughness.* New York: Vantage Press.

Gill, D. L., Dzewaltowski, D. A., & Deeter, T. E. (1988). The relationship of competitiveness and achievement orientation to participation in sport and nonsport activities. *Journal of Sport and Exercise Psychology, 10*, 139–150.

Glazer, S., Stetz, T. A., & Izso, L. (2004). Effects of personality on subjective job stress: A cultural analysis. *Personality and Individual Differences, 37*, 645–658.

Golby, J., & Sheard, M. (2004). Mental toughness and hardiness at different levels of rugby league. *Personality and Individual Differences, 37*, 933–942.

Golby, J., Sheard, M., & Lavallee, D. (2003). A cognitive-behavioural analysis of mental toughness in national rugby league football teams. *Perceptual and Motor Skills, 96*, 455–462.

Golby, J., & Sheard, M. (2006). The relationship between genotype and positive psychological development in national-level swimmers. *European Psychologist, 11*, 143–148.

Golby, J., Sheard, M., & van Wersch, A. (2007). Evaluating the factor structure of the Psychological Performance Inventory. *Perceptual and Motor Skills, 105*, 309–325.

Goldberg, A. S. (1998). *Sports slump busting: 10 steps to mental toughness and peak performance.* Champaign, IL: Human Kinetics.

Goodbody, J. (2002, May 18). Achieving greatness is all in the mind. *The Times*, p. 32 (Sport).

Goodbody, J. (2004a, August 20). Grobler demands toughness. *The Times*, p. 40 (Sport).

Goodbody, J. (2004b, August 27). Professional temptations kept away from Khan by protective Edwards. *The Times*, p. 50 (Sport).

Goodwill, V. (2007, January 24). Learning from mistakes is key to winning. *The Eastern Echo*. Retrieved January 24, 2007, from http://www.easternecho.com.

Gordon, P. (2007, October 19). Scotland can profit from Italian fear, says Strachan. *The Times*, p. 96 (Sport).

Gordon, P. (2009, February 7). Trent McClenahan in search of gold. *The Times*. Retrieved February 7, 2009, from http://www.timesonline.co.uk/tol/sport.

Gordon, S., Gucciardi, D., & Chambers, T. (2007). A personal construct theory perspective on sport and exercise psychology research: The example of mental toughness. In T. Morris, P. Terry, & S. Gordon (Eds.), *Sport psychology and exercise psychology: International perspectives* (pp. 43–55). Morgantown, WV: Fitness Information Technology.

Gorman, E. (2008a, March 15). Massa determined to give the flying Finn a run for his money. *The Times*, p. 8 (Formula One 2008).

Gorman, E. (2008b, November 3). Hamilton's lap of the gods. *The Times*, p. 76 (Sport).

Gould, D. (2002). Sport psychology in the new millennium: The psychology of athletic excellence and beyond. *Journal of Applied Sport Psychology, 14*, 137–139.

Gould, D., Dieffenbach, K., & Moffett, A. (2002). Psychological characteristics and their development in Olympic champions. *Journal of Applied Sport Psychology, 14*, 172–204.

Gould, D., Guinan, D., Greenleaf, C., Medbery, R., & Peterson, K. (1999). Factors affecting Olympic performance: Perceptions of athletes and coaches from more and less successful teams. *The Sport Psychologist, 13*, 371–394.

Gould, D., Hodge, K., Peterson, K., & Petlichkoff, L. (1987). Psychological foundations of coaching: Similarities and differences among intercollegiate wrestling coaches. *The Sport Psychologist, 1*, 293–308.

Graham, D., & Yocom, G. (1990). *Mental toughness training for golf.* Lexington, MA: Stephen Greene Press.

Grayling, A. C. (2001). *The meaning of things: Applying philosophy to life.* London: Weidenfeld & Nicolson.

Greenleaf, C. A., Gould, D., & Dieffenbach, K. (2001). Factors influencing Olympic performance: Interviews with Atlanta and Nagano U.S. Olympians. *Journal of Applied Sport Psychology, 13*, 179–209.

Greenwood, W. (2007, October 23). Springboks show real style. *The Daily Telegraph*, p. S14 (Sport).

Greenwood, W. (2009, February 21). England must grasp meaning of teamship. *The Daily Telegraph*, p. S16 (Sport).

Griffith, C. R. (1926). *Psychology of coaching.* New York: Scribner.

Griffith, C. R. (1928). *Psychology and athletics.* New York: Scribner.

Gucciardi, D. F., Gordon, S., & Dimmock, J. A. (2008). Towards an understanding of mental toughness in Australian football. *Journal of Applied Sport Psychology, 20*, 261–281.

Gucciardi, D. F., Gordon, S., & Dimmock, J. A. (2009). Development and preliminary validation of a mental toughness inventory for Australian football. *Psychology of Sport and Exercise, 10*, 201–209.

Hands, D. (2008a, May 7). Loffreda pleads for time to turn round Leicester from season of disappointment. *The Times*, p. 68 (Sport).

Hands, D. (2008b, November 3). Hook's nerveless kicking sneaks resilient Ospreys into semi-finals. *The Times*, p. 62 (Sport).

Hanrahan, S., Grove, J. R., & Lockwood, R. J. (1990). Psychological skills training for the blind athlete: A pilot program. *Adapted Physical Activity Quarterly*, *7*, 143–155.

Hans, T. (2000). A meta-analysis of the effects of adventure programming on locus of control. *Journal of Contemporary Psychotherapy*, *30*, 33–60.

Hansen, A. (2008, November 3). Gomes is one of worst I've seen. *The Daily Telegraph*, p. S13 (Sport).

Hanton, S., & Jones, G. (1999). The acquisition and development of cognitive skills and strategies: I. Making the butterflies fly in formation. *The Sport Psychologist*, *13*, 1–21.

Hardy, J., Gammage, K., & Hall, C. R. (2001). A description of athlete self-talk. *The Sport Psychologist*, *15*, 306–318.

Harman, N. (2008, January 21). Young Briton sent home for flagrant lapses of discipline. *The Times*, p. 69 (Sport).

Hattie, J., Marsh, H. W., Neill, J. T., & Richards, G. E. (1997). Adventure education and outward bound: Out-of-class experiences that make a lasting difference. *Review of Educational Research*, *67*, 43–87.

Hayward, P. (2003, November 24). England's heroes keep their feet on the ground. *The Daily Telegraph*, p. S2 (Sport).

Hayward, P. (2005, May 26). Bold Liverpool rise from the ashes. *The Daily Telegraph*, p. S3 (Sport).

Heishman, M. F., & Bunker, L. (1989). Use of mental preparation strategies by international elite female lacrosse players from five countries. *The Sport Psychologist*, *3*, 14–22.

Herbst, D. (1986). Nobody escapes pressure's clutches. *Bowlers Journal*, *73*, 90–94.

Hill, D. (2008, November 3). It takes mental strength to win a world title. *The Guardian*, p. 3 (Sport).

Hodge, K. (1994). Mental toughness in sport: Lessons for life. The pursuit of personal excellence. *Journal of Physical Education New Zealand*, *27*, 12–16.

Hodgkinson, M. (2008, January 21). British No2 junior sent home. *The Daily Telegraph*, p. S16 (Sport).

Hoedaya, D., & Anshel, M. H. (2003). Use and effectiveness of coping with stress in sport among Australian and Indonesian athletes. *Australian Journal of Psychology*, *55*, 159–165.

Hofstede, G. (1984). *Culture's consequences: International differences in work related values*. Beverly Hills, CA: Sage.

Hoggard, M. (2007, December 24). Why we failed to get ourselves out of sticky situations when the heat was on. *The Times*, p. 62 (Sport).

Hollander, D. B., & Acevedo, E. O. (2000). Successful English Channel swimming: The peak experience. *The Sport Psychologist, 14*, 1–16.

Holt, N. L., & Hogg, J. M. (2002). Perceptions of stress and coping during preparations for the 1999 women's soccer world cup finals. *The Sport Psychologist, 16*, 251–271.

Hopps, D. (2009, February 9). Time for Flower to make wilting England bloom. *The Guardian*. Retrieved February 9, 2009, from guardian. co.uk/sport.

Horsburgh, V. A., Schermer, J. A., Veselka, L., & Vernon, P. A. (2009). A behavioural genetic study of mental toughness and personality. *Personality and Individual Differences, 46*, 100–105.

Hotten, R. (2003, September 5). Football champs must learn mind games. *The Times*, p. 9.

Hoult, N. (2005, September 13). Head-to-head drives Flintoff and Warne to superstardom. *The Daily Telegraph*, p. S5 (Sport).

Hoult, N. (2008, August 21). Prior playing for keeps on England return. *The Daily Telegraph*, p. S20 (Sport).

Hughes, M. (2008, November 3). Search for perfect goal failing at final hurdle. *The Times*, p. 94 (Sport).

Hughes, R. H., & Coakley, J. (1991). Positive deviance among athletes: The implications of overconformity to the sport ethic. *Sociology of Sport Journal, 8*, 307–325.

Hughes, S. (2005a, September 13). Centurion Vaughan fulfils promise. *The Daily Telegraph*, p. VI (The Ashes 2005).

Hughes, S. (2005b, September 13). The day Trent Bridge held its breath. *The Daily Telegraph*, p. VII (The Ashes 2005).

Hughes, S. (2008, October 4). I lacked cut-throat edge for the big Test. *The Daily Telegraph*, pp. S12–S13.

Hutton, T. (2007, February 2). Nice guys finish first. *The Sun Sentinel*. Retrieved February 2, 2007, from http://www.sun-sentinel.com.

Hytner, D. (2008, August 8). Wenger underlines his faith in the young Gunners. *The Guardian*, p. 5 (Sport).

Hytner, D. (2009, March 14). Wenger's men scent victory in the battle for fourth. *The Guardian*, p. 5 (Sport).

Inverdale, J. (2007, November 21). "Blade runner" ruling should be heartless, not gutless. *The Daily Telegraph*, p. S13 (Sport).

Irvine, C. (2003, November 24). Ashes whitewash leaves Australia with something to crow about. *The Times*, p. 35 (Sport).

Irvine, C. (2007, October 11). Rhinos look to wild man to end St Helens streak. *The Times*, p. 79 (Sport).

Irvine, C. (2008a, July 5). Hanley's final mission is to turn tables for Doncaster. *The Times*, p. 102 (Sport).

Irvine, C. (2008b, October 5). Rhinos rule in the rain as Leeds win back to back titles. *The Times*. Retrieved October 5, 2008, from http://www.timesonline.co.uk/tol/sport.

Irvine, C. (2008c, October 6). Fierce Rhinos steamroller over farewell party for Anderson. *The Times*, p. 62 (Sport).

Irvine, C. (2009, April 10). Leon Pryce makes Wigan pay for letting lead slip. *The Times*, p. 78 (Sport).

Jackson, S. A. (1995). Factors influencing the occurrence of flow states in elite athletes. *Journal of Applied Sport Psychology*, *7*, 138–166.

Jackson, S. A., Mayocchi, L., & Dover, J. (1998). Life after winning gold: II. Coping with change as an Olympic gold medallist. *The Sport Psychologist*, *12*, 137–155.

Jenson, P. (2007, November 26). Capello swipe at McClaren. *The Times*, p. 2 (The Game).

Johnson, M. (2008, October 1). Battle on track will be even more intense in London. *The Daily Telegraph*, p. V5 (London 2012).

Jones, C. M. (1982, November). Mental toughness. *World Bowls*, pp. 30–31.

Jones, G., Hanton, S., & Connaughton, D. (2002). What is this thing called mental toughness? An investigation of elite sport performers. *Journal of Applied Sport Psychology*, *14*, 205–218.

Jones, G., Hanton, S., & Connaughton, D. (2007). A framework of mental toughness in the world's best performers. *The Sport Psychologist*, *21*, 243–264.

Jones, G., Hanton, S., & Swain, A. B. J. (1994). Intensity and interpretation of anxiety symptoms in elite and non-elite performers. *Personality and Individual Differences*, *17*, 657–663.

Jones, J. W., Neuman, G., Altmann, R., & Dreschler, B. (2001). Development of the Sports Performance Inventory: A psychological measure of athletic potential. *Journal of Business and Psychology*, *15*, 491–503.

Jones, S. (2008, March 9). Next step Grand Slam, then the world. *The Sunday Times*, p. 4 (Sport).

Joseph, J. (2008, January 29). Modern morals. *The Times*, p. 3 (Times2).

Kagan, J. (1999). Born to be shy? In R. Conlan (Ed.), *States of mind* (pp. 29–51). New York: Wiley.

Kahneman, D., Diener, E., & Schwartz, N. (Eds.). (1999). *Well-being: The foundations of hedonic psychology*. New York: Russell Sage.

Kang-Heon, L., Dongsung, S. S., Myung-Woo, H., & Elisa, L. (1994). Developing the norm of Korean table tennis players' mental toughness. *Korean Journal of Sport Science*, *6*, 103–120.

Kay, O. (2008, December 30). Oliver Kay Q&A: Steven Gerrard has the mental strength to cope. *The Times*. Retrieved December 30, 2008, from http://www.timesonline.co.uk/tol/sport.

Keohane, M. (2006, September 6). Losing is never a good habit. *News 24*. Retrieved September 7, 2006, from http://www.news24.com.

Kerr, J. H., Wilson, G. V., Bowling, A., & Sheahan, J. P. (2005). Game outcome and elite Japanese women's field hockey players' experience of emotions and stress. *Psychology of Sport and Exercise, 6*, 251–263.

Kervin, A. (2003, November 24). Woodward finds right answers on his day of judgment. *The Times*, p. 36 (Sport).

Khoshaba, D. M., & Maddi, S. R. (1999). Early experiences in hardiness development. *Consulting Psychology Journal: Practice and Research, 51*, 106–116.

Kierkegaard, S. (1959). *Either/Or* (D. F. Swenson & L. M. Swenson, Trans.). Garden City, NY: Doubleday. (Original work published 1843).

Kimmage, P. (2008, May 18). Talking with a straight bat. *The Sunday Times*, p. 19 (Sport).

Kirkcaldy, B. D. (1985). The values of traits in sport. In B. D. Kirkcaldy (Ed.), *Individual differences in movement* (pp. 257–277). Lancaster, England: MTP Press.

Kitson, R. (2008, November 17). Johnson's men fall well short of Wallabies when push comes to shove. *The Guardian*, pp. 10–11 (Sport).

Kitson, R. (2009, April 21). Physique comes first in naming of the Lions. *The Guardian*, p. 9 (Sport).

Kline, R. B. (2005). *Principles and practice of structural equation modelling* (2nd ed.). New York: Guilford.

Kobasa, S. C. (1979). Stressful life events, personality and health: An inquiry into hardiness. *Journal of Personality and Social Psychology, 37*, 1–11.

Kroll, W. (1967). Sixteen personality factor profiles of collegiate wrestlers. *Research Quarterly, 38*, 49–57.

Kuan, G., & Roy, J. (2007). Goal profiles, mental toughness and its influence on performance outcomes among Wushu athletes. *Journal of Sports Science & Medicine, 6*, 28–33.

Kuehl, K., Kuehl, J., & Tefertiller, C. (2005). *Mental toughness: A champion's state of mind*. Chicago, IL: Ivan R. Dee.

Kvist, J., Ek, A., Sporrstedt, K., & Good, L. (2005). Fear of re-injury: A hindrance for returning to sports after anterior cruciate ligament reconstruction. *Knee Surgery, Sports Traumatology, Arthroscopy, 13*, 393–397.

Lane, A. M. (2008). *Sport and exercise psychology*. London: Hodder Education.

Lane, A. M., Harwood, C., Terry, P. C., & Karageorghis, C. I. (2004).

Confirmatory factor analysis of the Test of Performance Strategies (TOPS) among adolescent athletes. *Journal of Sports Sciences, 22*, 803–812.

Lane, A. M., Thelwell, R., & Gill, G. (2007). Relationship between emotional intelligence and mental toughness. *Journal of Sports Sciences, 25*, 312–313.

Layard, R. (2006). *Happiness: Lessons from a new science*. London: Penguin.

LeDoux, J. (2002, August). The self and the brain. *Prospect, 77*, 50–53.

Lee, Y. T., Jussim, L., & McCauley, C. (1995). *Stereotype accuracy: Toward appreciating group differences*. Washington, DC: American Psychological Association.

Levy, A., Clough, P., Polman, R., Marchant, D., & Earle, K. (2005). Mental toughness and injury occurrence in elite swimming. *Journal of Sports Sciences, 23*, 1256–1257.

Levy, A., Polman, R. C. J., Clough, P. J., Marchant, D., & Earle, K. (2006). Mental toughness as a determinant of beliefs, pain, and adherence in sport injury rehabilitation. *Journal of Sport Rehabilitation, 15*, 246–254.

Lewis, D. (2008, August 20). Christine Ohuruogu's life will never be the same after this. *The Daily Telegraph*, p. S5 (Sport).

Lewsey, J. (2007, September 30). Colonial rant won't wilt the Red Rose. *The Sunday Times*, p. 18 (Sport).

Lewsey, J. (2009, January 31). Josh Lewsey's guide to the Six Nations teams. *The Daily Telegraph*. Retrieved January 31, 2009, from http://www.telegraph.co.uk/sport.

Ley, J. (2007, December 5). Wenger calls for reality check. *The Daily Telegraph*, p. S3 (Sport).

Lillee, D. (2003). *Lillee: An autobiography*. Sydney: Hodder.

Linley, P. A., & Joseph, S. (2004). Applied positive psychology: A new perspective for professional practice. In P. A. Linley & S. Joseph (Eds.), *Positive psychology in practice* (pp. 3–12). Hoboken, NJ: Wiley.

Lloyd, C. (2007, October 25). Lloyd orders restoration of work ethic after West Indies' fall from greatness. *The Times*, p. 90 (Sport).

Loe, R. (2007, October 14). Top two inches on missing list as Cup hopes buried. *New Zealand Herald*. Retrieved December 15, 2007, from http://www.nzherald.co.nz.

Loehr, J. E. (1986). *Mental toughness training for sports: Achieving athletic excellence*. Lexington, MA: Stephen Greene Press.

Loehr, J. E. (1995). *The new toughness training for sports*. New York: Plume.

Lord, C. (2007, November 19). All that glitters is gold for America's man on a mission: Phelps's formula for greatness in the pool. *The Times*, p. 70 (Sport).

Luckner, J. L., & Nadler, R. S. (1997). *Processing the experience: Strategies to enhance and generalize learning*. Dubuque, IA: Kendall Hunt.

Luszki, W. A. (1982). *Winning tennis through mental toughness*. New York: Everest House.

Lyles, C. (2008, August 3). Ramps in hundred club at last. *The Observer*, p. 4 (Sport).

Lynch, R. (2008, November 19). Robinson lashes out at "unprepared" England. *The Guardian*. Retrieved November 19, 2008, from http:// www.guardian.co.uk/sport.

Lyubomirsky, S. (2001). Why are some people happier than others? The role of cognitive and motivational processes in well-being. *American Psychologist, 56*, 239–249.

Mack, M. G., & Ragan, B. G. (2008). Development of the mental, emotional, and bodily toughness inventory in collegiate athletes and nonathletes. *Journal of Athletic Training, 43*, 125–132.

Macrae, C. N., Stangor, C., & Hewstone, M. (1996). *Stereotypes and stereotyping*. New York: Guilford.

Maddi, S. R. (1990). Issues and interventions in stress mastery. In H. S. Friedman (Ed.), *Personality and disease* (pp. 121–154). New York: Wiley.

Maddi, S. R. (2004). Hardiness: An operationalization of existential courage. *Journal of Humanistic Psychology, 44*, 279–298.

Maddi, S. R. (2006). Hardiness: The courage to grow from stresses. *Journal of Positive Psychology, 1*, 160–168.

Maddi, S. R., Harvey, R. H., Khoshaba, D. M., Lu, J. L., Persico, M., & Brow, M. (2006). The personality construct of hardiness, III: Relationships with repression, innovativeness, authoritarianism, and performance. *Journal of Personality, 74*, 575–597.

Maddi, S. R., Kahn, S., & Maddi, K. L. (1998). The effectiveness of hardiness training. *Consulting Psychology Journal: Practice and Research, 50*, 78–86.

Maddi, S. R., & Khoshaba, D. M. (2001). *Personal Views Survey* (3rd ed., rev.). Newport Beach, CA: The Hardiness Institute.

Maddi, S. R., Khoshaba, D. M., Persico, M., Lu, J., Harvey, R., & Bleecker, F. (2002). The personality construct of hardiness: II. Relationships with comprehensive tests of personality and psychopathology. *Journal of Research in Personality, 36*, 72–85.

Mahoney, C. A., & Todd, M. K. (1999). Cross-cultural comparison of psychological skills in college-aged soccer players. *Journal of Sports Sciences, 17*, 59–60.

Mairs, G. (2006, October 6). Harrison's the head man. *The Belfast Telegraph*, p. 1 (Sport).

Malin, I. (2008, September 1). Tributes and tears for Sculthorpe, man of fractured steel. *The Guardian*, p. 14 (Sport).

Malthouse, M. (2008, May 23). Retirement plays out in the mind before body surrenders. *The Australian*. Retrieved August 30, 2008, from http://www.theaustralian.com.au/sport.

Marchant, D., Clough, P., Polman, R., Levy, A., & Strycharczyk, D. (2007, March). *Employees' mental toughness is associated with their managerial position and age*. Poster session presented at the annual meeting of the British Psychological Society, York, England.

Marsh, H. W. (1997). The measurement of physical self-concept: A construct validation approach. In K. Fox (Ed.), *The physical self: From motivation to well-being* (pp. 27–58). Champaign, IL: Human Kinetics.

Martens, R. (2004). *Successful coaching* (3rd ed.). Champaign, IL: Human Kinetics.

Martindale, R. J. J., Collins, D., & Abraham, A. (2007). Effective talent development: The elite coach perspective in UK sport. *Journal of Applied Sport Psychology, 19*, 187–206.

McDonald, M. (2008, August 5). Knights make bid for finals. *The Australian*. Retrieved August 30, 2008, from http://www.theaustralian.com.au/sport.

McKay, J., Niven, A. G., Lavallee, D., & White, A. (2008). Sources of strain among elite UK track athletes. *The Sport Psychologist, 22*, 143–163.

McKenzie, M. D. (2000). How are adventure education program outcomes achieved? *Australian Journal of Outdoor Education, 5*, 19–28.

McRae, D. (2008, January 19). Humble heavyweight Skelton aims for the shock of all ages. *The Guardian*, p. 8 (Sport).

McRae, D. (2009, January 27). I dream up things and then convince myself they're possible. *The Guardian*. Retrieved January 27, 2009, from http://www.guardian.co.uk/sport.

Meir, R. A., McDonald, K. N., & Russell, R. (1997). Injury consequences from participation in professional rugby league: A preliminary investigation. *British Journal of Sports Medicine, 31*, 132–134.

Meyers, A. W., Whelan, J., & Murphy, S. (1995). Cognitive behavioral strategies in athletic performance enhancement. In A. Meyers, J. Whelan, & S. Murphy (Eds.), *Progress in behavior modification* (pp. 137–164). Pacific Grove, CA: Brooks/Cole.

Meyers, M. C., Bourgeois, A. E., LeUnes, A., & Murray, N. G. (1998).

Mood and psychological skills of elite and sub-elite equestrian athletes. *Journal of Sport Behavior*, *22*, 399–409.

Meyers, M. C., LeUnes, A., & Bourgeois, A. E. (1996). Psychological skills assessments and athletic performance in collegiate rodeo athletes. *Journal of Sport Behavior*, *19*, 132–146.

Middleton, S. C., Marsh, H. W., Martin, A. J., Richards, G. E., & Perry, C. (2004a, July). Discovering mental toughness: A qualitative study of mental toughness in elite athletes. In G. E. Richards (Chair), *High performing athletes: Self-concept and achievement goals*. Symposium conducted at the meeting of the International Conference on Self-concept, Motivation and Identity: Where to go from here? Berlin, Germany.

Middleton, S. C., Marsh, H. W., Martin, A. J., Richards, G. E., & Perry, C. (2004b, July). *Developing the Mental Toughness Inventory (MTI)*. Poster session presented at the meeting of the International Conference on Self-concept, Motivation and Identity: Where to go from here? Berlin, Germany.

Middleton, S. C., Marsh, H. W., Martin, A. J., Richards, G. E., Savis, J., Perry, C., et al. (2004c). The Psychological Performance Inventory: Is the mental toughness test tough enough? *International Journal of Sport Psychology*, *35*, 91–108.

Miles, J. C., & Priest, S. (Eds.). (1990). *Adventure education*. State College, PA: Venture.

Miller, P. S., & Kerr, G. A. (2002). Conceptualizing excellence: Past, present, and future. *Journal of Applied Sport Psychology*, *14*, 140–153.

Mischel, W., & Shoda, Y. (1995). A cognitive-affective system theory of personality: Reconceptualizing situations, dispositions, dynamics, and invariance in personality structure. *Psychological Review*, *102*, 246–268.

Moore, B. (2007, October 15). World-class Wilkinson thrives under pressure. *The Daily Telegraph*, p. S3 (Sport).

Moore, B. (2009, April 13). Pressure zone shows the real winners. *The Daily Telegraph*, p. S17 (Sport).

Moran, A. (2004). *Sport and exercise psychology: A critical introduction*. Hove, England: Routledge.

Mulvenney, N. (2007, January 23). Defeat raises more questions about Li's mental toughness. *The Guardian*. Retrieved January 23, 2007, from http://www.guardian.co.uk/sport.

Murray, E. (2009, February 13). "Farcical assumptions made after Old Firm matches," says Smith. Retrieved February 13, 2009, from http://www.guardian.co.uk/sport.

Nadler, R. S. (1993). Therapeutic process of change. In M. A. Gass (Ed.),

Adventure therapy: Therapeutic applications of adventure programming (pp. 57–69). Dubuque, IA: Kendall Hunt.

Neill, J. T., & Dias, K. L. (2001). Adventure education and resilience: The double edged sword. *Journal of Adventure Education and Outdoor Learning, 1*, 35–42.

Neill, J. T., & Richards, G. E. (1998). Does outdoor education really work? A summary of recent meta-analyses. *Australian Journal of Outdoor Education, 3*, 2–9.

Nicholas, M. (2005, September 13). Centurion Vaughan fulfils promise. *The Daily Telegraph*, p. VI (The Ashes 2005).

Nicholas, M. (2007, December 24). India need strength of mind and body. *The Daily Telegraph*, p. S31 (Sport).

Nicholas, M. (2008, January 21). Sharma magic casts a spell. *The Daily Telegraph*, p. S24 (Sport).

Nicholls, A. R., Holt, N. L., & Polman, R. C. J. (2005). A phenomenological analysis of coping effectiveness in golf. *The Sport Psychologist, 19*, 111–130.

Nicholls, A. R., Holt, N. L., Polman, R. C. J., & Bloomfield, J. (2006). Stressors, coping, and coping effectiveness among professional rugby union players. *The Sport Psychologist, 20*, 314–329.

Nicholls, A. R., Polman, R. C. J., Levy, A. R., & Backhouse, S. H. (2008). Mental toughness, optimism, pessimism, and coping among athletes. *Personality and Individual Differences, 44*, 1182–1192.

Noblet, A. J., & Gifford, S. M. (2002). The sources of stress experienced by professional Australian footballers. *Journal of Applied Sport Psychology, 14*, 1–13.

Noblet, A., Rodwell, J., & McWilliams, J. (2003). Predictors of the strain experienced by professional Australian footballers. *Journal of Applied Sport Psychology, 15*, 184–193.

Norris, E. K. (1999). *Epistemologies of champions: A discursive analysis of champions' retrospective attributions: Looking back and looking within*. Michigan, MI: Michigan University Microfilms International.

O'Connor, A. (2003, November 24). Serial winners finally learn how to become good losers. *The Times*, p. 39 (Sport).

O'Connor, D. M. (2004). Groin injuries in professional rugby league players: A prospective study. *Journal of Sports Sciences, 22*, 629–636.

Ogden, M. (2008, November 3). Arsenal "lack spine" for title chase. *The Daily Telegraph*, p. S14 (Sport).

Old, J. (2004). Organisational behaviour in sport organisations. In J. Beech & S. Chadwick (Eds.), *The business of sport management* (pp. 69–92). London: Pearson.

Orlick, T., & Partington, J. (1988). Mental links to excellence. *The Sport Psychologist*, *2*, 105–130.

Pain, M. A., & Harwood, C. G. (2004). Knowledge and perceptions of sport psychology within English soccer. *Journal of Sports Sciences*, *22*, 813–826.

Pankey, B. (1993). Presence of mind: Five ways to lower your class drop-out rate with mental toughness. *American Fitness*, *11*, 18–19.

Pargman, D. (Ed.). (1999). *Psychological bases of sport injuries*. Morgantown, WV: Fitness Information Technology, Inc.

Parkinson, M. (2004). Courage of our favourite Aussie. Tribute to Keith Miller: Wartime hero adored in England was ranked with the best all-rounders of all-time. *The Daily Telegraph*, p. 8 (Sport).

Parkinson, M. (2005). In *England's Ashes* (p. 7). London: HarperSport.

Patrick, H. (2008, October 5). Leeds beat St Helens to win Super League Grand Final at Old Trafford. Retrieved October 5, 2008, from http://www.telegraph.co.uk/sport.

Peabody, D. (1985). *National characteristics*. New York: Cambridge University Press.

Pérusse, L., Rankinen, T., Rauramaa, R., Rivera, M. A., Wolfarth, B., & Bouchard, C. (2003). The human gene map for performance and health-related fitness phenotypes: The 2002 update. *Medicine and Science in Sports and Exercise*, *35*, 1248–1264.

Peterson, C., & Seligman, M. E. P. (2004). *Character strengths and virtues: A handbook and classification*. Washington, DC: American Psychological Association.

Philip, R. (2004, August 30). Kelly sprints to pre-eminence. *The Daily Telegraph*, p. S5 (Sport).

Plomin, R., DeFries, J. C., McClearn, G. E., & McGuffin, P. (2001). *Behavioral genetics* (4th ed.). New York: Worth.

Podlog, L., & Eklund, R. C. (2007). Professional coaches' perspectives on the return to sport following serious injury. *Journal of Applied Sport Psychology*, *19*, 207–225.

Preston, E. (2008, July, 8). It's tough, it's lonely and it's ruthless as you move up, Robson warned. *The Guardian*, p. 5 (Sport).

Priest, S., & Gass, M. A. (2005). *Effective leadership in adventure programming* (2nd ed.). Champaign, IL: Human Kinetics.

Pringle, D. (2005, September 13). It's business as usual at HQ. *The Daily Telegraph*, p. II (The Ashes 2005).

Pringle, D. (2009, February 16). Strauss century leads revival. *The Daily Telegraph*, p. S1 (Sport).

Privette, G., & Bundrick, C. M. (1997). Psychological processes of peak, average, and failing performance in sport. *International Journal of Sport Psychology*, *28*, 323–334.

Puni, A. C. (1963). Psihologicheskaya podgotovka sportsmena k sorevnovaniyu [Psychological preparation of athletes for a competition]. *Theory and Practice of Physical Culture*, *2*, 52–56.

Randall, C. (2008, January 21). England lacking grit indoors. *The Daily Telegraph*, p. S27 (Sport).

Ray, R., & Wiese-Bjornstal, D. M. (1999). *Counseling in sports medicine*. Champaign, IL: Human Kinetics.

Reason, M. (2009a, April 5). Padraig Harrington's major success is mainly in the mind. *The Daily Telegraph*. Retrieved April 5, 2009, from http://www.telegraph.co.uk/sport.

Reason, M. (2009b, April 14). In the agony of defeat, Perry proves himself a real winner. *The Daily Telegraph*, p. S13 (Sport).

Reed, T. (2007, December 13). Every loser wins. *MSN UK News*. Retrieved December 13, 2007, from http://www.news.uk.msn.com.

Rees, P. (2007, October 15). So now the best preparation is not to prepare at all. *The Guardian*, p. 4 (Sport).

Rees, P. (2008, March 13). Gatland brings best out of new-model Henson. *The Guardian*, p. 11 (Sport).

Reiss, M. (2006, September 27). One step at a time: Fellow kickers advise patience with rookie Gostkowski. *The Boston Globe*. Retrieved September 27, 2006, from http://www.boston.com.

Rich, T. (2008, September 30). Arsenal desperate to clear their heads. *The Daily Telegraph*, p. S2 (Sport).

Ridley, M. (2003). *Nature via nurture: Genes, experience and what makes us human*. London: Harper Perennial.

Robinson, L. (1999). Following the quality strategy – the rationale for the use of quality programmes. *Managing Leisure: An International Journal*, *4*, 201–217.

Robinson, L. (2003). The business of sport. In B. Houlihan (Ed.), *Sport and society: A student introduction* (pp. 165–183). London: Sage.

Roebuck, P. (2006, December 6). Old masters discover a new lease of life. *The Independent*, p. 57 (Sport).

Roper, M. (2007, December 3). Saracens show rivals their winning mentality even in defeat. *The Daily Telegraph*, p. S23 (Sport).

Rotter, J. B. (1954). *Social learning and clinical psychology*. Englewood Cliffs, NJ: Prentice Hall.

Rowan, P. (2009, April 12). Niko Kranjcar's late strike eases Portsmouth's woes. *The Sunday Times*. Retrieved April 12, 2009, from http://www.timesonline.co.uk/tol/sport.

Rushton, J. P., Bons, T. A., & Hur Y.-M. (2008). The genetics and evolution of a general factor of personality. *Journal of Research in Personality, 42*, 1173–1185.

Rushton, J. P., & Irwing, P. (2009). A general factor of personality in the Comrey Personality Scales, the Minnesota Multiphasic Personality Inventory-2, and the Multicultural Personality Questionnaire. *Personality and Individual Differences, 46*, 437–442.

Rutter, M. (1987). Psychosocial resilience and protective mechanisms. *American Journal of Orthopsychiatry, 57*, 316–331.

Rutter, M. (1999). Resilience concepts and findings: Implications for family therapy. *Journal of Family Therapy, 21*, 119–144.

Ryan, M. (2005, December 9). From Ashes to dust [Letter to the editor]. *The Daily Telegraph*, p. S10 (Sport).

Saferstein, D. (2005). *Win or lose: A guide to sports parenting*. Ann Arbor, MI: Trusted Guide Press.

Saferstein, D. (2006). *Strength in you: A student-athlete's guide to competition and life*. Ann Arbor, MI: Trusted Guide Press.

Saleeby, D. (Ed.). (1997). *The strength perspective in social work practice* (2nd ed.). New York: Longman.

Scarnati, J. T. (2000). Beyond technical competence: Developing mental toughness. *Career Development International, 5*, 171–176.

Scheier, M. F., Carver, C. S., & Bridges, M. W. (1994). Distinguishing optimism from neuroticism (and trait anxiety, self-mastery, and self-esteem): A reevaluation of the life orientation test. *Journal of Personality and Social Psychology, 67*, 1063–1078.

Schmid, J., & Leiman, J. M. (1957). The development of hierarchical factor solutions. *Psychometrika, 22*, 53–61.

Schoel, J., Prouty, D., & Radcliffe, P. (1988). *Islands of healing: A guide to adventure based counselling*. Hamilton, MA: Project Adventure, Inc.

Schoon, I., & Bartley, M. (2008, January). The role of human capacity and resilience. *The Psychologist*, 24–27.

Schwartz, S. H. (1994). Beyond individualism/collectivism: New cultural dimensions of values. In U. Kim, H. C. Triandis, Ç. Kâgitçibasi, S. Choi, & G. Yoon (Eds.), *Individualism and collectivism: Theory, method, and applications* (pp. 85–119). Thousand Oaks, CA: Sage.

Segall, M. H., Dasen, P. R., Berry, J. W., & Poortinga, Y. H. (1999). *Human behaviour in global perspective: An introduction to cross-cultural psychology* (2nd ed.). Boston, MA: Allyn and Bacon.

Seligman, M., & Csikszentmihalyi, M. (2000). Positive psychology: An introduction. *American Psychologist, 55*, 5–14.

Shafer, A. B. (1999). Factor analyses of Big Five Markers with the Comrey Personality Scales and the Howarth Personality Tests. *Personality and Individual Differences, 26*, 857–872.

Sheard, M. (2003, June 27). How not to win at Wimbledon [Letter to the editor]. *The Times*, p. 25 (Comment).

Sheard, M. (2006, December 6). Testing times [Letter to the editor]. *The Times*, p. 18 (Comment).

Sheard, M. (2008a, July). *Personality hardiness distinguishes elite-level sport performers*. Poster session presented at the meeting of the 29th International Congress of Psychology, Berlin, Germany.

Sheard, M. (2008b, July). *Construct validation of the alternative Psychological Performance Inventory (PPI-A) and the Sports Mental Toughness Questionnaire (SMTQ)*. Poster session presented at the meeting of the 14th European Conference on Personality, Tartu, Estonia.

Sheard, M. (2009). Hardiness commitment, gender, and age differentiate university academic performance. *British Journal of Educational Psychology*, *79*, 189–204.

Sheard, M. (in press). A cross-national analysis of mental toughness and hardiness in elite university rugby league teams. *Perceptual and Motor Skills*.

Sheard, M., & Golby, J. (2006a). Effect of a psychological skills training program on swimming performance and positive psychological development. *International Journal of Sport and Exercise Psychology*, *4*, 149–169.

Sheard, M., & Golby, J. (2006b). The efficacy of an outdoor adventure education curriculum on selected aspects of positive psychological development. *Journal of Experiential Education*, *29*, 187–209.

Sheard, M., & Golby, J. (2007a, March). *Psychological characteristics that identify elite level sport performers: The moderating role of hardiness*. Poster session presented at the annual meeting of the British Psychological Society, York, England.

Sheard, M., & Golby, J. (2007b). Hardiness and undergraduate academic study: The moderating role of commitment. *Personality and Individual Differences*, *43*, 579–588.

Sheard, M., & Golby, J. (2008, September). *Resisting stress in sports officiating: The moderating role of positive psychology*. Poster session presented at the meeting of the 14th World Congress of Psychiatry, Prague, Czech Republic.

Sheard, M., & Golby, J. (2009). Investigating the "rigid persistence paradox" in professional rugby union football. *International Journal of Sport and Exercise Psychology*, *6*, 101–114.

Sheard, M., & Golby, J. (in press). Personality hardiness differentiates elite-level sport performers. *International Journal of Sport and Exercise Psychology*.

Sheard, M., Golby, J., & van Wersch, A. (2009). Progress toward construct validation of the Sports Mental Toughness Questionnaire (SMTQ). *European Journal of Psychological Assessment, 25,* 184–191.

Simpson, R. J., Gray, S. C., & Florida-James, G. D. (2006). Physiological variables and performance markers of serving soldiers from two "elite" units of the British Army. *Journal of Sports Sciences, 24,* 597–604.

Slack, T., & Hinnings, B. (1992). Understanding change in national sports organisations: An integration of theoretical perspectives. *Journal of Sport Management, 6,* 114–132.

Slot, O. (2005, June 2). Injury report highlights danger zones for elite English players. *The Times,* p. 87 (Sport).

Slot, O. (2007a, October 13). England told to search for hero inside themselves. *The Times,* p. 120 (Sport).

Slot, O. (2007b, October 15). Ashton's film buffs barely able to believe their own box-office hit. *The Times,* p. 80 (Sport).

Smith, E. (2009, February 21). Strauss becomes a leader by example. *The Daily Telegraph,* p. S15 (Sport).

Smith, R. E. (2006). Understanding sport behaviour: A cognitive-affective processing systems approach. *Journal of Applied Sport Psychology, 18,* 1–27.

Smith, R. E., & Smoll, F. L. (1989). The psychology of "mental toughness": Theoretical models and training approaches to anxiety reduction in athletes. In C. C. Teitz (Ed.), *Scientific foundations of sport medicine* (pp. 391–402). Philadelphia, PA: B. C. Decker.

Smith, R. E., & Smoll, F. L. (2002). *Way to go, coach! A scientifically-proven approach to coaching effectiveness* (2nd ed.). Portola Valley, CA: Warde.

Smithies, T. (2007, January 23). Jets work on mind games. *The Daily Telegraph (Australia).* Retrieved January 23, 2007, from http://www.news.com.au/dailytelegraph.html.

Smoll, F. L., & Smith, R. E. (2005). *Sports and your child: Developing champions in sports and in life* (2nd ed.). Palo Alto, CA: Warde.

Snow, M. (2008, August 17). The taking part? Pah! *The Sunday Times,* p. 32 (Life & Style).

Snyder, A. W. (1999, June-July). Mind, body, performance. *Olympic Review,* 71–74.

Soderstrom, M., Dolbier, C., Leiferman, J., & Steinhardt, M. (2000). The relationship of hardiness, coping strategies, and perceived stress to symptoms of illness. *Journal of Behavioral Medicine, 23,* 311–328.

Souster, M. (2003, November 24). Jones generous in defeat after pre-match attrition. *The Times,* p. 35 (Sport).

Souster, M. (2007, October 15). Backbone of England with spirit of a bulldog. *The Times,* p. 72 (Sport).

Souster, M. (2009, March 30). Rampant Bristol delay the inevitable. *The Times*, p. 62 (Sport).

Spiers, G. (2008a, January 31). Ferguson on target to put Rangers into final. *The Times*, p. 96 (Sport).

Spiers, G. (2008b, March 29). McCoist: "We now have a toughness, an ability to win games". *The Times*, p. 108 (Sport).

Starkes, J. L., Weir, P. L., Singh, P., Hodges, N. J., & Kerr, T. (1999). Aging and the retention of sport expertise. *International Journal of Sport Psychology*, *30*, 283–301.

Stead, D. (2003). Sport and the media. In B. Houlihan (Ed.), *Sport and society* (pp. 184–200). London: Sage.

Strelan, P., & Boeckmann, R. J. (2006). Why drug testing in elite sport does not work: Perceptual deterrence theory and the role of personal moral beliefs. *Journal of Applied Social Psychology*, *36*, 2909–2934.

Stuart, L. (2008, February 29). Macfadyen puts his injury woes behind him to focus on return. *The Times*, p. 85 (Sport).

Stuart, L. (2009, March 14). Three reasons for Scotland to have hope. *The Times*. Retrieved March 14, 2009, from http://www.timesonline.co.uk/tol/sport.

Syed, M. (2007, October 15). Heroes? No, just men doing their job. *The Times*, p. 71 (Sport).

Syed, M. (2009a, February 4). Nadal's priceless gift to Federer – defeat. *The Times*, p. 59 (Sport).

Syed, M. (2009b, February, 11). Giggs knows path to greatness has no end. *The Times*, p. 71 (Sport).

Tabachnick, B. G., & Fidell, L. S. (2007). *Using multivariate statistics* (5th ed.). Boston, MA: Allyn & Bacon.

Taniguchi, S., & Freeman, P. A. (2004). Outdoor education and meaningful learning: Finding the attributes to meaningful learning experiences in an outdoor education program. *Journal of Experiential Education*, *26*, 210–211.

Taylor, J. (1989). Mental toughness (Part 2): A simple reminder may be all you need. *Sport Talk*, *18*, 2–3.

Tenenbaum, G., Fogarty, G., Stewart, E., Calcagnini, N., Kirker, B., Thorne, G., et al. (1999). Perceived discomfort in running: Scale development and theoretical considerations. *Journal of Sports Sciences*, *17*, 183–196.

Terracciano, A., Abdel-Khalek, A. M., Ádám, N., Adamovová, L., Ahn, C.-k., Ahn, H.-n., et al. (2005). National character does not reflect mean personality trait levels in 49 cultures. *Science*, *310*, 96–100.

The England Cricket Team. (2005). *Ashes victory*. London: Orion.

Thelwell, R., Weston, N., & Greenlees, I. (2005). Defining and understanding mental toughness within soccer. *Journal of Applied Sport Psychology, 17*, 326–332.

Thelwell, R. C., Weston, N. J. V., & Greenlees, I. A. (2007). Batting on a sticky wicket: Identifying sources of stress and associated coping strategies. *Psychology of Sport and Exercise, 8*, 219–232.

Thomas, P. R., Murphy, S. M., & Hardy, L. (1999). Test of performance strategies: Development and preliminary validation of a comprehensive measure of athletes' psychological skills. *Journal of Sports Sciences, 17*, 697–711.

Thomas, P. R., & Over, R. (1994). Psychological and psychomotor skills associated with performance in golf. *The Sport Psychologist, 8*, 73–86.

Thomas, P. R., Schlinker, P. J., & Over, R. (1996). Psychological and psychomotor skills associated with prowess at ten-pin bowling. *Journal of Sports Sciences, 14*, 255–268.

Thompson, J. (2003). *The double-goal coach: Positive coaching tools for honouring the game and developing winners in sports and life.* New York: Harper Information.

Tibbert, S., Morris, T., & Andersen, M. (2009). Mental toughness and recovery in athletes. *Journal of Science and Medicine in Sport, 12S*, S33.

Tillich, P. (1952). *The courage to be.* New Haven, CT: Yale University Press.

Tomase, J. (2007). Beating Chargers left players feeling super. *The Boston Herald.* Retrieved January 24, 2007, from http://www.patriots.boston-herald.com.

Tongue, S. (2008, June 27). Fabregas: "Our mental strength has been the key". *The Independent*, p. 70 (Sport).

Tremayne, P., & Tremayne, B. (2004). Children and sport psychology. In T. Morris & J. Summers (Eds.), *Sport psychology: Theory, applications and issues* (2nd ed., pp. 529–546). Milton, Australia: Wiley.

Tugade, M. M., & Fredrickson, B. L. (2004). Resilient individuals use positive emotions to bounce back from negative emotional experiences. *Journal of Personality and Social Psychology, 86*, 320–333.

Tunney, J. (1987). Thoughts on the line. Mental toughness: Biceps for the mind. *Soccer Journal, 32*, 49–50.

Turner, B. (2007, July 31). Happiness is . . . being Danish and enjoying life. *The Times*, p. 8 (Times2).

Tutko, T. A., Lyon, L. P., & Ogilvie, B. C. (1969). *Athletic Motivation Inventory.* San Jose, CA: Institute for the Study of Athletic Motivation.

Tutko, T. A., & Richards, J. W. (1972). *Coach's practical guide to athletic motivation.* Boston, MA: Allyn & Bacon.

Tutko, T. A., & Richards, J. W. (1976). *Psychology of coaching.* Boston, MA: Allyn & Bacon.

Vadocz, E. A., Hall, C., & Moritz, S. E. (1997). The relationship between competitive anxiety and imagery use. *Journal of Applied Sport Psychology*, *9*, 241–252.

Vallée, C. N., & Bloom, G. A. (2005). Building a successful university program: Key and common elements of expert coaches. *Journal of Applied Sport Psychology*, *17*, 179–196.

Vallerand, R. J., Blanchard, C. M., Mageau, G. A., Koestner, R., Ratelle, C., Léonard, M., et al. (2003). Les passions de l'âme: On obsessive and harmonious passion. *Journal of Personality and Social Psychology*, *85*, 756–767.

Vallerand, R. J., & Miquelon, P. (2007). Passion for sport in athletes. In D. Lavallee & S. Jowett (Eds.), *Social psychology in sport* (pp. 249–262). Champaign, IL: Human Kinetics.

Van den Heever, Z., Grobbelaar, H. W., & Potgieter, J. C. (2007). A survey of psychological skills training in South African netball. *African Journal for Physical, Health Education, Recreation and Dance*, *13*, 254–266.

Vealey, R. S. (1994). Current status and prominent issues in sport psychology interventions. *Medicine and Science in Sports and Exercise*, *26*, 495–502.

Wallston, K. A. (1989). Assessment of control in health-care settings. In A. Steptoe & A. Apple (Eds.), *Stress, personal control, and health* (pp. 85–101). Chichester, England: Wiley.

Walsh, D. (2007, October 21). Accidental heroes. *The Sunday Times*, p. 6 (Sport).

Walsh, D. (2008a, February 24). Ashton's battling bruisers punch above their weight. *The Sunday Times*, p. 2 (Sport).

Walsh, D. (2008b, November 16). Arsenal title challenge fades after 2–0 defeat by Villa. *The Sunday Times*, p. 1 (Sport).

Walsh, D. (2009, March 29). Paul O'Connell: Warren Gatland and me. *The Sunday Times*. Retrieved March 29, 2009, from http://www.timesonline.co.uk/tol/sport.

Warne, S. (2008, September 29). Pietersen can become the best batsman in the world. *The Times*, pp. 66–67 (Sport).

Watson, D., Clark, L. A., & Tellegen, A. (1988). Development and validation of brief measures of positive and negative affect: The PANAS scales. *Journal of Personality and Social Psychology*, *54*, 1063–1070.

Watts, F. N., Webster, S. M., Morley, C. J., & Cohen, J. (1992). Expedition stress and personality change. *British Journal of Psychology*, *83*, 337–341.

Waugh, S. (2006). *Out of my comfort zone*. Camberwell, Australia: Penguin.

Werner, A. C., & Gottheil, E. (1966). Personality development and participation in collegiate athletics. *Research Quarterly, 37*, 126–131.

Westerby, J. (2008, December 9). Aaron Mauger relishes Dan Carter reunion. *The Times.* Retrieved December 9, 2008, from http://www.timesonline.co.uk/tol/sport.

Westman, M. (1990). The relationship between stress and performance: The moderating effect of hardiness. *Human Performance, 3*, 141–155.

Whitmarsh, B. G., & Alderman, R. B. (1993). Role of psychological skills training in increasing athletic pain tolerance. *The Sport Psychologist, 7*, 388–399.

Wiebe, D. J. (1991). Hardiness and stress moderation: A test of proposed mechanisms. *Journal of Personality and Social Psychology, 60*, 89–99.

Wilkinson, J. (2008). *Tackling life.* London: Headline.

Wilkinson, M., & Ashford, B. (1997). Psychological profiling and predictive validity. *Journal of Sports Sciences, 15*, 111.

Williams, J. M., & Krane, V. (2001). Psychological characteristics of peak performance. In J. M. Williams (Ed.), *Applied sport psychology: Personal growth to peak performance* (4th ed., pp. 162–178). Mountain View, CA: Mayfield.

Williams, R. (2003, November 24). A new set of heroes – and even Australia agrees. *The Guardian*, p. 2.

Williams, R. M. (1988). The U.S. Open character test: Good strokes help. But the most individualistic of sports is ultimately a mental game. *Psychology Today, 22*, 60–62.

Wilson, A. (2008, October 6). Smith and Leeds rewarded for persistence with sweetest of prizes. *The Guardian*, pp. 10–11 (Sport).

Wilson, A. (2009a, February 23). Long helps make short work of Giants. *The Guardian*, p. 14 (Sport).

Wilson, A. (2009b, April 9). Pryce takes Saints back to the top but Wigan close the gap. *The Guardian.* Retrieved April 9, 2009, from http://www.guardian.co.uk/sport.

Wilson, C., Edwards, D., & Collins, T. (2005). Long-term rider development. Retrieved September 20, 2008, from http://www.sportscoachuk.org.

Wilson, G. V., & Kerr, J. H. (1999). Affective responses to success and failure: A study of winning and losing in competitive rugby. *Personality and Individual Differences, 27*, 85–89.

Wilson, J. (2007, November 26). England role could be tempting, says Klinsmann. *The Daily Telegraph*, pp. S2–S3 (Sport).

Wilson, J. (2009, February 23). Lampard reveals his debt to Ranieri ahead of reunion. *The Daily Telegraph*, p. S5 (Sport).

Winter, H. (2005, May 27). How Liverpool defied belief. *The Daily Telegraph*, p. S2 (Sport).

Winter, H. (2006, September 5). England have mindset to survive Balkan cauldron. *The Daily Telegraph*, p. 3 (Sport).

Winter, H. (2007, November 26). Peril awaits on Eastern Front. *The Daily Telegraph*, p. S2 (Sport).

Winter, H. (2009, March 31). "Today's kids have it too easy": Lampard says pampered young players should go back to cleaning the senior professionals' boots. *The Daily Telegraph*, p. 51 (Sport).

Woods, R., Hocton, M., & Desmond, R. (1995). *Coaching tennis successfully*. Champaign, IL: Human Kinetics.

Young, E. (2001, March 30). Mind game: Psychological superiority alone could explain why Australia has won every rugby league World Cup since 1975. Retrieved April 10, 2001, from http://www.newscientist.com.

Zuckerman, M. (2005). *Psychobiology of personality* (2nd ed.). New York: Cambridge University Press.

Index